Helen Trenos
Creativity: the Actor in Performance

Published by De Gruyter Open Ltd, Warsaw/Berlin
Part of Walter de Gruyter GmbH, Berlin/Munich/Boston

© 2014 Helen Trenos
ISBN: 978-3-11-040210-0
e-ISBN: 978-3-11-040196-7

Bibliographic information published by the Deutsche Nationalbibliothek
The Deutsche Nationalbibliothek lists this publication in the Deutsche Nationalbibliografie; detailed bibliographic data are available in the Internet at http://dnb.dnb.de.

Managing Editor: Monika Michałowicz

www.degruyteropen.com

Cover illustration: © ThinkStock/andreusK

Helen Trenos

Creativity: The Actor in Performance

Managing Editor: Monika Michałowicz

DE GRUYTER OPEN

For David

Contents

List of CREATICS Exercises

Introduction

Why another book about acting? Isn't there already a plethora of actor-training methodologies and manuals fighting for centre-stage, tripping over each other to upstage the rest? The question is rhetorical and the answer is yes. But rarely do any of them address the full gamut of the actor's creativity. This is the rationale for this book: an approach to actor training aimed at developing actors' creativity not for the workshop, classroom or rehearsal (which are all well catered for) but in and for *performance*.

Creativity: the Actor in Performance had its genesis as soon as I graduated from drama school, some twenty years ago. Like most fledgling actors, I entered the profession simultaneously starry eyed and terrified: '*Was I really talented enough? Did I have what it takes?*' I stilled my anxiety with the knowledge that I had enjoyed, without question, a comprehensive training at one of Australia's most prestigious acting conservatories (The Western Australian Academy of Performing Arts). Although I was well aware upon graduating that there was still much I had to learn, I felt confident that my three-year training had covered most bases. So despite the niggling reservations, it was with this confidence that I entered the profession. Mine was a dream debut, landing an agent and a lead role in an exciting new work for a major company. I was on my way, and in my first years as a professional actor I was fortunate to play a variety of roles. Spanning the West's classical canon to contemporary works, I acted across a range of styles from psychological realism to non-naturalism, and performed in a broad cross-section of theatrical contexts. In these early days of my career everything seemed to be progressing swimmingly. I was getting good feedback from my directors and peers and—what is the bottom line—I was getting work. But, in spite of this apparent success, I knew deep down that something crucial was lacking, as if a key part of the jigsaw was missing. Again and again, after each performance, I would be left with a feeling of dissatisfaction. I felt as if I were trapped inside a paper bag— stifled and unable to punch my way through.

At first, I thought that this 'barrier', this sense of 'not getting through' in performances might stem from inadequate character-work. Perhaps I was not identifying with my characters closely enough. So I worked even harder on my characterisations, dissecting my script into ever more beats and objectives (using an even greater array of coloured highlighter pens) and delving even further into my characters: '*What music would Masha listen to? What books would she read? What did she eat for breakfast? Did she eat breakfast?*' When, and not surprisingly, this didn't seem to help, I thought I had possibly become overly preoccupied with character details. Maybe with all this focus on character, I was not being open enough to my fellow-actors and all that was going on around me on the rehearsal floor. I, therefore, worked toward being more vulnerable and open in rehearsals. But none of these attempts at a solution got rid of the sense of alienation I continued to experience in performance. I just couldn't fight my way out of that damned paper bag.

Eventually a more productive reason surfaced, one which emerged out of my observations of successful actors—not on the rehearsal room floor, but in performance. These were actors who were esteemed by their peers, directors and, most crucially, by their audiences. Two actors especially come to mind. One was, like me, an emerging actor and the other a well-seasoned veteran, and although they came from vastly different training backgrounds and had very different approaches to their work, I noted that they had one thing in common: they were deliciously seductive. Audiences could not resist them. Watching them, you were drawn in, hooked, as if there were an invisible cord connecting you. They could be thrilling, propel you forward to the edge of your seat, force the hairs on the back of your neck to bristle and there were moments when they could make the space explode. This was not done in a crude way. Rather, what they did was subtle—in fact, so subtle that it was not immediately apparent to me *what* they were doing. What was apparent, however, was that while they were not necessarily better *actors* than me, they were superior *performers*.

This realisation surprised me. After all, hadn't my Stanislavsky-based training equipped me with all that was needed for drawing in an audience? If I focussed on achieving my character objectives and connected with my fellow-actors wouldn't I automatically engage the audience? That is what Tortsov, Stanislavsky's fictional teacher in *An Actor Prepares* and *Building a Character*, tells his acting students:

> If actors really mean to hold the attention of a large audience they must make every effort to maintain an uninterrupted exchange of feelings, thoughts and actions among themselves. And the inner material for this exchange should be sufficiently interesting to hold spectators (Stanislavsky, 1964).

Yet, in my experience, this 'inner material', the intercourse between actors, was not enough. I, for instance, was very good at establishing and maintaining contact with my fellow actors, but I felt that I was still not engaging with my audiences as consistently and wholeheartedly as I would have liked and as I had observed in my two role models. Evidently something *extra* was needed. What it was I did not know, but I did have my question, my goal, my agenda:

What is this extra something it takes to engage an audience and be effective both in the rehearsal room and in performance? Is it innate? Do you either have it or not? Can it be taught?

Over my twenty-year acting career, I probed these questions, continuing to observe other actors at work as well as 'sitting on my own shoulder', scrutinizing my own work. Eventually, I decided to take some time out and devoted five years to investigating this *something extra*. In fact, I completed a Masters Degree and PhD on the subject. If this sounds obsessive, then it was. But it was worth it: investigating that *special something* needed in performance led me to a much more fundamental and important question: *what is the creativity of acting?*

What I discovered is that the actor's creativity is much richer and its scope broader than is commonly held. There are two distinct contexts in which actors are called upon to be creative: *rehearsal* and *performance*. Self-evident though this may seem, it is a distinction seldom made in acting theories. Elly Konijn makes the observation that:

> Common acting theories usually do not make a clear distinction between rehearsal and performance. Usually they describe a rehearsal method to reach an accurate portrayal. These methods barely touch on acting in performance (Konijn, 2002).

Nor are the differences between acting in rehearsal and acting in performance made in most standard actor-training institutes and programs. There is an overwhelming focus in Western mainstream actor training on the creative processes of actors in *rehearsals* collaborating with *directors* in order, primarily, to create *characters*. The actor's work in *performance,* collaborating with *audiences*, is rarely (if ever) addressed and if it is, the assumption is made that being creative in rehearsals will automatically translate into successful performances. This, however, is not necessarily so. There are those actors who are spectacular in rehearsal but fail to achieve the promise they showed there in their performances—where it counts. Why? Because acting in performance requires something different, something beyond that which is required or acquired in rehearsal, no less than a new creative act. Ask any actor waiting backstage to make their first entrance. As you wait in the wings, whispering your lines to drown the thumping in your chest or humming quietly to yourself to keep the voice warmed and the nerves steadied--you are acutely aware that the instant you set foot on stage, in front of an audience, something is going to have to happen beyond anything that occurred in rehearsal. *This* is not merely an extension of rehearsals, an end point of a process that began with the script—*this* is a new act of creation where they, the actors, are primary creators—for and with their co-conspirators, the audience. And *this* requires techniques, strategies and skills which differ from those practised in rehearsals.

Creativity: the Actor in Performance fills this gap in current actor training, nurturing the actor's creativity beyond rehearsals, beyond working with directors, and beyond characterisations. These areas are all well covered by current actor training methodologies, but over the years I have developed a series of exercises and strategies aimed at enhancing the actor's creativity in performance. These I have called *CREATICS*. Derived from the adjective *creatic* ('of or pertaining to the flesh'), I chose the name because it simultaneously suggests both creativity and the bodily presence of the actor in performance. As such, *CREATICS* is designed not to replace but to complement existing actor training methodologies. I teach my students, for example, Stanislavsky, Chekhov and Viewpoints, but through *CREATICS* exercises and strategies, I extend these training regimes into acting in performance.

Chapters 1 to 3 of *Creativity: the Actor in Performance* provide an historical and theoretical rationale for a performance-oriented training. In Chapter 4, the basis for a performance-oriented methodology is outlined along with some sample exercises. *CREATICS'* exercises can be successfully used working on scenes in workshops, rehearsals and throughout the performance season. It is my strong belief that actor training should not stop once opening night has come and gone, rather it is vital that the teaching and learning extend into the run when actors can use their performance experiences as impetus for ongoing training and development.

1 Creativity and Acting

On Australia Day 2004, I was tuned into a TV show called *The Greatest Australian*. The program featured a panel of eminent Australians in fields ranging from 'the arts to the sciences, from sport to show business' and their task on this night was 'to convince the nation of their choice of The Greatest Australian' (King, 2004). According to the 'promo', the program promised 'to entertain, delight and surprise'. Surprise it did. A pleasant surprise was that theatre was represented in its own right. David Williamson, arguably Australia's most prolific and successful playwrights, was one of the panelists. The not so pleasant surprise came when his fellow panelist, Jackie Frank (founding editor of *Marie Claire* magazine) blackballed Nicole Kidman. In Frank's view, Nicole could not be in the running because (I waited for the answer with bated breath), she is *just* an actor and as an actor she is not 'creating work in her own right'. While nobody on the panel (not even Williamson) batted an eyelid, my world stopped and in this hiatus I screamed into the void: 'If Nicole Kidman is not creative, then what is she doing out there? And what have I been doing for the last twenty years?'

While Frank's remarks roused me to the edge of my seat, what got me up on my feet was the simultaneous awareness that—aside from acting, so it seemed—creativity was beginning to be found everywhere. Creative acts were becoming ubiquitous. Creativity was occurring from the boardroom (*Management and Creativity: from creative industries to creative management*) to the bedroom (*Sex 101: Over 350 Creative Ways to a Godly, Loving, Pleasurable Marriage*), and was pertinent to a growing number of human endeavours: scrapbooking (*Creativity Tips for Scrapbookers*), bricklaying (*Creative Brickwork*), religion (*Jesus and Creativity*), and even divorce (*The New Creative Divorce*). Amazon yielded a staggering 355,163 references in English to 'creative' or 'creativity' in book titles. There was no question about it, creativity had in the closing decade of the twentieth century become a buzzword and growth industry, and it continues to be so. Perceived as a desirable personal attribute, integral to notions of self-development and expression, social and cultural success and even economic survival, it has become the province of potentially all people in a growing range of domains, and associated with an increasing array of activities. Our paradigms for creativity may have once been derived from the arts and sciences, but this has radically changed. Robert Weiner, who has written extensively on the subject, correctly observes that now 'all we need do is look at the telephone listings' to discover that the traditional domains of creativity 'are just a fraction of the spheres' in which it is evoked' (Weiner, 2000). Historian John Hope Mason is right to claim that during the course of the twentieth century an ever-increasing 'number of human attributes came to be crowned with the laurel wreath of creativity' (Hope Mason, 2003).

Acting, however, was not one of them. Why not? As an actor, I had no doubt that I performed a creative act on stage, so why deny actors the 'laurel wreath of creativity'?

Questions kept forming in my mind, until I came upon the two that would insti-
gate my research: *What exactly is the creativity of acting?* And, for that matter, *what
is creativity?*

1.1 Creativity: Emergence of the Concept

'*In contemporary culture, no idea is so appealing, no word put to more frequent and
varied use than creativity*' (Barzun, 1991).

Despite the fact that men and women have obviously exercised their creativity since,
at least, the first recorded cave paintings some thirty thousand years ago, the actual
word *creativity* is a surprising newcomer to the English language. *The Oxford English
Dictionary* dates the first recorded use as 1875 and attributes it to English historian
A.W. Ward, who wrote of Shakespeare's 'poetic creativity' (*OED* 'Creativity').

Creativity had its predecessors—*creator, create, creation*. However, these words
were not applied to human endeavours until the latter part of the fifteenth century.
Tracing the etymological lineage, the earliest recorded usage in the thirteenth century
was unequivocal: *creator = God*. Creator is, and can only be, the 'Supreme Being who
creates all things' (*OED* 'Creator' Def.1). Almost one hundred years on, the verb *create*
and its product or activity *creation* emerged and reinforced the power of the divine
Creator: to *create* could only ever be '[s]aid of the divine agent' ('Create' Def. 1a), and
'creation' describes 'the action of bringing into existence by divine power' ('Creation'
Def. 1a). In 1592, poet and playwright John Davies did not mince words: to 'create, to
God alone pertains' ('Create' Def. 1c). But Davies was on shaky ground: by the close
of the sixteenth century, such a sentiment had become less convincing, and in the
ensuing centuries, people's faith in their own power and creative abilities gathered
momentum. By the second half of the sixteenth century the big 'C' Creator conceded
the existence of small 'c' creators and creations, and this is reflected in the new definitions emerging at this time:
- *create*: 'To make, form, constitute, or bring into legal existence (an institution,
  condition, action, mental product, or form, not existing before)' ('Create' Def. 2a);
- *creation*: 'The action of making, forming, producing, or bringing into existence'
  ('Creation' Def. 2a);
- *creator*: 'One who, or that which, creates or gives origin to' ('Creator' Def. 2a).

Why this shift came about was arguably because of events occurring in Western Europe
during the fifteenth and sixteenth centuries: in particular, the political upheavals of
the Reformation and the unprecedented technological and cultural changes of the
Renaissance. During the Reformation, *who* might assume the title of *creator* here on
Earth remained contentious. One could speculate that the emergence of temporal
uses of *create* was partly born out of the contest between the Church and State which

resulted in the ceding of power—and the power to *create*—from Pope to kings and then trickling down to princes, dukes, members of parliament until, eventually, creativity becomes the province of all. Running parallel to this, certain events of the Renaissance both bolstered belief in human creativity and boosted its value. Scientific discoveries and technological advances radically altered people's world views and, not to be overlooked, was the emergence of a commercial class across Europe: bankers, merchants, and traders were at this time financing, selling, and trading the usefully innovative. This enlarged scope still did not evoke human creativity as it is conceived today, but it had moved a considerable step closer. When Shakespeare wrote in the midst of the Renaissance: 'Are you a god? Would you create me new?' (*The Comedy of Errors* 3.ii.40)—it could be rhetorical, but it could also be a direct question.

It is not surprising, therefore, that in the late seventeenth century the adjective *creative* appears and defines a positive, *human* attribute: 'the quality of creating, given to creating; of or pertaining to creation; originative' ('Creative' Def. 1a). To be creative soon became integral to the simultaneously emerging concepts of 'individuality' and 'freedom'. By the close of the eighteenth century, Coleridge was arguing that 'to develop the powers of the Creator is our proper employment' (Coleridge, 1795/1971). In the mid-nineteenth century, Matthew Arnold was adamant: it 'is undeniable that the exercise of a creative power, that a free creative activity, is the highest function of man' (Arnold, 1865/1968).

Adjectives have a need for nouns; attributes require sources, origins. So, shortly after Arnold extolled the benefits and virtues of being *creative*, a new noun—*creativity*—comes onto the scene. This is the most interesting step in the etymological evolution: from *creative* a new—putative source—is extrapolated, *creativity*. Weiner makes the point that, for the first time, with the advent of this abstract noun, 'attention could be directed to a phenomenon, capacity, or characteristic noticeable in many dimensions of human endeavour' (Weiner, 2000). One should be cautious, however, of normalizing what is presented as 'natural'. Creativity, we must remind ourselves, is an abstraction. In fact, it is a classic example of hypostatization, whereby a noun is derived from referring a series of actions to a purported source. Having thus been postulated, 'it' must now be located and made 'real', and this is precisely what then occurred. In the early twentieth century, Alfred North Whitehead and the Process philosophers took the first step, reifying *creativity* as an epistemological principle which was so radical that it transcends even God. In *Process and Reality*, Whitehead writes that creativity is 'the universal of universals characterizing ultimate matter of fact' (Whitehead, 1929).

But, it was not until the 1950s that the decisive developments occurred: American Psychology co-opted creativity, located it in particular *psychological qualities of the individual*, and made it popular.

Finally, thanks to Psychology, *creativity* entered our vernacular.

1.2 Psychology and Creativity

'is creativity a property of people, products or processes?' (Mayer, 1999).

Psychology folklore has it that, following his address to the American Psychological Association in 1950, J. P. Guilford (the APA president), 'almost single-handedly' rallied support for creativity, which was until then described as 'one of psychology's poor orphans' (Sternberg & O'Hara, 1999; Sternberg & Lubart, 1999). From this watershed event, American Psychology led the research into creativity, establishing as early as the 1960s its own journals devoted to the subject: *The Journal of Creative Behavior* and *Creativity Research Journal*. Psychology's research has focussed on defining creativity by endeavouring to locate its source: is it found in *people* and their personalities or cognitive *processes*, or is creativity located in *products?*

1.2.1 The Creative Product

The creative *product* provided Psychology with the basis for defining creativity. Teresa Amabile makes the point that 'most explicit definitions have used the creative product as the distinguishing sign of creativity' (Amabile, 1983). Moreover, there was an overwhelming consensus within Psychology that the creative product, and therefore creativity itself, had two defining criteria: *novelty* and *value*. Mayer claims unequivocally that the 'majority endorses the idea that creativity involves the creation of an original and useful product' (Mayer, 1999). Wallace and Gruber concur: like 'most definitions of creativity, ours includes novelty and value. The creative product must be new and must be given value according to some external criteria' (Wallace & Gruber, 1989). Sternberg and Lubart comment that creativity 'is the ability to produce work that is both novel (i.e. original, unexpected) and appropriate (i.e. useful, adaptive concerning task and constraints)' (Sternberg & Lubart, 1999). Amabile argues that a 'product or response will be judged as creative to the extent [...] it is both a novel and appropriate, useful, correct or valuable response to the task at hand' (Amabile, 1983). Finally, Hausman, speaking from outside Psychology, claims that 'an act that is creative must, in a special way, be controlled and must yield a product which is valuable and new with respect to its Structure and Form' (Hausman, 1984).

However, these criteria are clearly too broad: on its own admission, sixty years after Psychology set itself the task of saying what creativity is, it is no closer to a definition based on product. Mayer is unequivocal: an 'important challenge for the next fifty years of creativity research is to develop a clearer definition of creativity' (Mayer, 1999). Sternberg echoes this: 'the definition and criteria of creativity are a matter of ongoing debate' (Sternberg, 2003), and Boden concedes that there 'are fundamental conceptual difficulties in saying what creativity *is*' (Boden, 2004).

Attempts to analyse the creative *product* have not provided Psychology with a clear definition of creativity, nor has the *product* proved to be creativity's source. Creative products—the artefacts, texts, ideas, theories, performances, discoveries and so forth which creativity yields—might be evidence of creativity occurring, but they are not in themselves generators of creativity. Logically, before we have a creative product, there must be *somebody* creating it. Psychology therefore turned its attention to the creative *person*—his or her personality or cognitive processes. Given Psychology's disciplinary focus, this was a natural move. However, before moving on to the creative *person*, let's return, for a moment, to the question of the creativity of acting and ask: what is the creative *product* of acting?

If the painter creates a painting, the poet a poem, the sculptor a sculpture, the playwright a play, and so forth, then what does the actor create? Following the formula, it would appear to be an *action* or *act*. Yet several other answers also come to mind: *character, emotion, audience response*, just to name a few. The answer to what constitutes the creative product of acting is crucial, for it determines how acting and its creativity are defined. It also informs how we train actors. If, for example, the creative product of acting is considered to be *character*, then the training is focused on character-creation and acting is judged in terms of characterisation: how *true-to-life, convincing, complex, consistent with the playwright's fictional character* may just be a few of the criteria used to assess the actor's success and creativity.

On the other hand, if the creative product of acting is deemed to be *performance*, then other criteria come into play: *is the performance well paced? Is it suspenseful when necessary? Does it hold the spectators' attention? Did it elicit gasps of rapturous response? Is it clear? Can the actors be seen and heard?...*

'What is the creative product of acting?'—proves to be a useful question and one I frequently put to my students. Nine times out of ten the answer I get is: '*Characters. It's obvious, isn't it? Acting is about creating characters.*' Not without reason is this the common reply. After all, our hegemonic acting style is psychological realism, which is character-driven. However, with a little further questioning, other responses surface as acting students come to realise that while they do create characters, they create much more and to restrict acting to characterisation is to short-change its creativity.

1.2.2 The Creative Personality

Psychology has focussed its energy on defining the creative personality and identifying those traits that, putatively, make a person creative. To do this, researchers have taken high-profile creators and extrapolated their personality traits. These have then become the defining characteristics of *the* creative personality.

There are, however, problems with this approach. The supposed traits are too numerous and varied to be of any definitive use. The research has yielded such an unwieldy array of personality traits that they are rendered invalid as a useful set of descriptors. In her 'Pyramid of Talent Development', for instance, Jane Piirto lists the following personality traits: 'drive', 'passion', 'self-discipline', 'intuition', 'curiosity', 'openness', 'naivety', 'imagination', 'risk-taking', 'perception', 'insight', 'tolerance for ambiguity', 'perfectionism', 'volition', 'resilience', 'androgyny', 'persistence', 'over-excitability', 'intellect', 'emotion', 'imagination', 'sensuality' and 'creativity' itself (Piirto, 2005). Plucker and Renzulli list: 'awareness of their creativity', 'originality', 'independence', 'risk-taking', 'personal energy', 'curiosity', 'humour', 'attraction to complexity and novelty', 'artistic sense', 'open-mindedness', 'need for privacy', 'heightened perception' and 'a tolerance for ambiguity' (Plucker & Renzulli, 1999). Dean Keith Simonton includes 'motivation', a 'creative cognitive style', 'relative intro-version' and a 'high degree of independence and autonomy' (Simonton, 2005). It would appear from these traits, that when it comes to the creative personality, almost anything goes.

Moreover, from the earliest personality-trait research there were contradictions in the findings. In 1931, Joseph Rossman identified 'self-confidence' as a characteris-tic of the creative personality, whereas in the same year, William Hirst distinguished 'bashfulness' and 'over-sensitivity' (Melrose, 1989). Apart from such contradictions, there exists the questionable assumption that people are either one or the other, but not both. It assumes that in all situations people will consistently display one trait and not its opposite, whereas empirical evidence reveals that people are frequently both—depending on the situation or the stage of the creative process. Mihaly Csik-szentmihalyi makes the point that 'persons are characterized not so much by single traits. [...] They are not just introverted, but can be both extroverted and introverted, depending on the phase of the [creative] process' (Csikszentmihalyi, 1999). The way around this paradox is to argue that the creative personality can be both, but this has brought Psychology no nearer to a definition of the creative personality as such.

Beyond these objections, there is a fundamental fallacy to this 'eminent person-ality' approach: entrapment in a classic hermeneutic circle. Any personality traits which define the creative personality must themselves be derived from a precon-ceived notion of what these traits are. This preconceived notion, however, must have already been derived from the traits it now purports to establish. So around we go in a hermeneutic circle...

As neither the creative product nor the person has led Psychology closer to the source of creativity, it has turned to the last member of the triumvirate—the creative *process*, specifically cognitive processes, how creative people think. But before ven-turing there, I would like to once more take the lead from Psychology and pose the question: Is the creativity of acting to be found in the *personality* of the actor?

Playwright Louis Nowra suggests that actor Judy Davis's 'dark' and 'obnoxious personality'—a 'combination of self-loathing and narcissism and haughty ego'—is necessary fuel for her prodigious talent (Nowra, 2004). One of Australia's leading actors' agents, Bill Shanahan, thought that 'neurosis' was the 'special ingredient' a good actor should possess (Trengrove, 1991). Within Psychology's research, some attention has been given to creativity as located in the actor's personality—or more accurately, their neuroses. A prominent study by Hammond and Edelman in 1991 found that professional actors scored significantly higher on the neuroticism scale than did non-actor subjects (Feist, 1999). In the view of psychologist Otto Fenichel, the actor is at heart an exhibitionist who in acting fulfills 'a certain erogenous' and 'narcissistic satisfaction' and whose greatest anxiety is 'castration fear'. Sensitive creatures, actors require 'success on stage [...] in the same way as milk and affection are needed by the infant' (Fenichel, 1960). Most actors I know would find all of this amusing, and it is little more than that. Not surprisingly, studies on the personality of actors have yielded no useful data and to reduce the actor's creativity to neuroses, or even personality, is reductive, denying the complexity of acting.

1.2.3 The Creative Process

Research into the creative process can be traced back to the nineteenth century: the first process model of creativity is attributed to Hermann von Helmholtz (1896), who examined his own creative process and elicited three stages: investigation, rest, and a sudden, unexpected solution. Over the years, these three stages have been refined and added to. In 1926, Graham Wallas expanded on the basic model: preparation, incubation, illumination, and verification (Melrose, 1989). By the 1970s, MacKinnon had outlined the following stages:
- 'preparation'—this involves the 'experience' and 'cognitive skills' necessary to ask the right question or pose the correct problem;
- 'effort' required to solve the problem;
- 'withdrawal' from the problem to allow it to incubate;
- 'moment of insight'—the Eureka moment;
- 'verification, evaluation, elaboration and the application of insight' (MacKinnon, 1976).

Then, in the late 1980s, Howard Gruber added two more stages to the model: 'expansive application' and 'problem-finding' (Gruber, 1989).

Yet, while process models might provide a useful starting point for thinking about creativity, it is self-evident that creativity does not occur in neat, sequential stages. Rather, when creating you often hurdle over a stage to a later stage and frequently move back and forward. Graham Wallas made the qualification that the 'stages', far from being discrete and progressing in order, 'constantly overlap each other' (Wallas, 1926).

Following suit, acting cannot be reduced to a simple, linear process. Applying MacKinnon's five-stage model, however, provokes some intriguing insights into the creativity of acting and its scope:
1. *Preparation*: actors identify the problems they may incur in realizing their roles;

2. *Effort:* they work at home and in rehearsal to find solutions;
3. *Withdrawal:* if solutions are not forthcoming, they let the problems incubate;
4. *Moment of insight:* in the middle of the night, on the bus, under the shower a solution suddenly becomes apparent;
5. *Verification of insight:* they take this solution into the rehearsal room and test it, hoping the director will say: 'You hit it today!'

But where does *performance* come into this? Is it just an extension of rehearsals? Does the actor take what was agreed to in rehearsals and reproduce it in performance—or does performance herald a new creative process? Something like this:

1. *Preparation:* actors identify and anticipate potential problems, moment to moment;
2. *Effort:* without time for reflection, solutions must be instantaneous;
3. *Withdrawal:* there is no time for problems to incubate;
4. *Moment of insight:* actors must hit on a solution—or fail!
5. *Verification of insight:* there is no time for testing the solution—it succeeds or fails in the moment it is enacted and received by the audience.

In performance, in other words, actors embark on a completely different—and scary—creative process! Robert Keith Sawyer, in fact, asks whether 'it is appropriate to represent creativity in sequential stages', suggesting that acting in performance challenges this notion. The 'insight' or Eureka stage is not necessarily distinct from the final evaluation or verification stage. He makes the interesting point that if this is the case in performing, then these stages may be indistinguishable in other forms of creativity as well (Sawyer, 2005).

If that is one caveat regarding Psychology's process theories, the greater problem has been the collapsing of creativity into problem-solving. In an attempt to demystify creativity, researchers have equated mental processes associated with solving simple, everyday problems with creativity. Weisberg suggests that 'thought processes involved in artistic creativity are of the same sort as [...] ordinary individuals solving simple problems' (Weisberg, 1986). Margaret Boden claims, creativity 'is not a special 'faculty' but an aspect of human intelligence [...] grounded in everyday abilities such as conceptual thinking, perception, memory and reflective self-criticism' and, subsequently, 'every one of us is creative' (Boden, 2004). Also for Mayer, creativity is 'a general skill or trait or characteristic that can be applied to a wide variety of situations' (Mayer, 1999). Smith, Ward and Finke assert that 'creative thinking encompasses special combinations and patterns of the same cognitive processes seen in other noncreative endeavors' (Smith, Ward & Finke, 1995). A creativity which is defined as problem-solving is compelled to include even the most banal activities within its rubric. According to Weisberg: 'getting dressed, taking a shower, cooking a meal, or starting a car are all potentially creative, and, more radically, 'all behavior involves novelty at its core' (Weisberg, 1986).

Arguably, this is the biggest legacy of American Psychology's creativity research: creativity conceived as problem-solving and, therefore, ubiquitous. Throughout its history, we have seen that creativity has become increasingly democratic and Psychology has taken it to the ultimate point where creativity is *everywhere* and potentially *everybody* is creative. The problem with such a conception is that definitional boundaries dissolve, rendering creativity meaningless.

The research question driving Psychology's creativity research—is creativity located in products, people or processes?—has not yielded convincing answers. Psychology has attempted to address these failures by conceiving of creativity as coming from a number of sources, a confluence of variables, including environment. This has marked a positive shift in Psychology's research and is reinforced by the relatively more recent investigations undertaken by Anthropology, whose enterprise to broaden the tight focus on the creative individual is a breath of fresh air. The conveners of the Association of Social Anthropologists 2005 conference ('Creativity and Cultural Improvisation') comment that in recent years a number of approaches have been developed that 'bring into critical focus the limitations entailed in conceptualizing creativity as a form of invention exercised by the autonomous individual' (Ingold & Hallam, 2007). Within Anthropology, creativity is commonly conceived not only as 'a property of individuals' but also of 'social situations'—and inter*actions* (Lavie, Narayan & Rosaldo, 1993).

The emphasis on *action* is decisive: Psychology's research has been overwhelmingly on what creativity *is*, but perhaps creativity *is* what it *does*. Logically, this would appear to be the case: before you can have a creative product, Psychology maintains that there must be a creative person—the individual with *the* 'right' personality and mental processes, situated in the 'right' environment. But it is possible that this person could have all the 'right' variables to deem them creative, but not actually create anything. So we either resign ourselves to the notion that creativity is defined by a certain *je ne sais quoi*, a certain 'it' factor that we cannot define or locate, or we investigate the creative *act*. And, surely, the logic leads us here: before the creative person, there must be a creative act. The person can only be defined as creative by the act of creation. Creativity is not a question of who a person is or where they come from, but what he/she does. Jung famously remarked: 'It is not Goethe who creates *Faust*, but *Faust* which creates Goethe' (Ghiselin, 1952). Logically, he is correct: a creator cannot pre-exist, but is born in and by the creative act: if there is no creative act, there is no creator or creation.

The creative *act* has been investigated by psychologist and creativity researcher Robert Keith Sawyer, who has turned to none other than *acting* as the focus of his research. He makes the point that acting 'is a relatively new topic of creativity' (Sawyer, 2005). This attention is long overdue, according to Sawyer, because acting has the potential to enrich existing conceptions of creativity. He observes:

> Acting has three characteristics that make it uniquely valuable to creativity researchers: it emphasizes the creative process, rather than the creative product; it is usually created by a collaborative ensemble; and it emphasizes spontaneity (Sawyer, 2005).

Surprisingly, within Theatre discourse, there is little literature which explicitly interrogates the creativity of acting. For example, Hardie and Arnita Albright's, *Acting, the Creative Process* (1980) and Ramon Delgado's, *Acting with Both Sides of Your Brain: Perspectives on the Creative Process* (1988) are based on unquestioned assumptions, namely that the creativity of acting is completed by the creation of characters and that there is little (if any) difference between the creative processes of actors working in rehearsal and performance. A survey of some major theatre journals yields no articles which *explicitly* explore the topic. While they may allude to the creativity of acting, or refer to it in passing, it is never the primary focus.

It can, of course, be argued that implicit in every theory and methodology of acting is a conception of what constitutes its creative element. For instance, Zinder's excellent book *Body, Voice & Imagination* draws on the exceptional work of Michael Chekhov and shares his 'fascination of the creative moment as it unfolds in the time/ space of performance' (Zinder, 2009). However, questioning what actually constitutes the creativity of acting is not Zinder's mission. In *The Moving Body: Teaching Creative Theatre*, Jacques Lecoq presumes without question that the actor's creativity is an 'abstract dimension, made up of spaces, lights, colours, materials, sounds' which is 'laid down in all of us by our various experiences and sensations' (Lecoq, 2002). And, as I discuss in Chapter 3, Stanislavsky, who unequivocally championed the actor's creativeness, did not question the legitimacy of its definitions in prevailing trends. In fact, the volume of literature directly addressing the creativity of acting is very limited, and the assumptions underpinning definitions of the stage actor's creativity are rarely—if ever—questioned.

This brings me back to the 'Frank factor'. Possibly, the paucity of rigorous enquiry in the West into the creativity of stage acting has its source and ongoing frustration in a *mis*conception—the widespread belief that *acting is simply not creative.*

1.3 Is Acting Creative?

'[The labor of creativity] cannot be likened to that of the actor and the instrumentalist. [...] They too strain, but only in order to realize a model, not to create something out of nothing' (Dufrenne, 1983).

Denying the creativity of acting is part of what Jonas Barish has identified as a broader anti-theatre prejudice, dating back to Plato. In the *Ion*, the rhapsode is not only 'portrayed as a foolish posturing fellow, naively vain of his talent', but he 'ranks lower in the scale of truth than the painter, sculptor, or poet, for where they are interpreters, he is but 'the [interpreter] of interpreters' (Barish, 1981). While throughout the course of history, the painter, sculptor and poet have all been promoted from interpreters to originators, the actor has not. Actors might 'strain', according to French philosopher Mikel Dufrenne, but they do not create *ex-nihilo*. Yet, is it possible for anyone 'to create something out of nothing'? Shakespeare's Lear identifies the logical flaw inherent in such a concept of creativity: '[n]othing will come of nothing' (*King Lear* 1. i. 92). The problem, in other words, lies not in the actor, but in this (mis)definition of creativity. Creating something from nothing, outside of Heaven, is impossible. In *The Act of Creation*, Arthur Koestler writes:

> The creative act is not an act of creation in the sense of the Old Testament. It does not create something out of nothing; it uncovers, selects, reshuffles, combines, synthesizes already existing facts, ideas, faculties, skills (Koestler, 1970).

If the defining characteristic of creativity were the production of the uniquely *original* then there would be *no* creative artists, actors or otherwise. *Ex-nihilo* creation does not and cannot exist—all that exists is uncovering, reshuffling, combining, synthesizing, *interpreting* that which is already there. One can, thus, reverse the charge: *all artists are interpretative*—just like actors.

Other similar objections to acting derived from careless or faulty definitions of creativity can be similarly dismissed.

1.3.1 Acting is Everywhere

'*Any one can walk and talk and look and gesticulate*' Edward Hugh Sothern (Cole & Chinoy, 1970).

Acting's supposed ubiquity is often put forward as an obstacle to its being conceived as creative. Performing and, by association, acting have infiltrated almost all facets of everyday life, and while this proliferation of acting/performing metaphors has, to some degree, served to position theatre favourably and influentially in relation to other discourses, the paradox is that it has simultaneously contributed to the devaluing of acting as a creative art. If performing and acting can be used to describe how we function in our everyday lives—then not only are they ubiquitous, but what is more damaging to the status of acting as an art form—anybody can do it. Today this is given even more credence by the fact that TV, especially soaps, routinely cast untrained, inexperienced 'actors'. Apart from the suffering caused by exposure to frequently poor performances, such practices perpetuate the myth that acting is not an art with its own craft—a view with historical precedence. In 1888, theatre critic William Archer wrote in *Masks or Faces* that we 'are all actors in rudiment, the tendency to such imitation being part of the mechanism of animated nature'. This is the reason why, according to Archer, 'the stage is besieged by incompetent aspirants, the general tendency being easily mistaken for special aptitude'. Archer is correct in distinguishing between the acting which is everywhere, done by everybody in everyday situations—the innate 'general tendency'—and the acting which is an art with its own body of skills—the 'special aptitude'. Aptitude in itself, however, is not enough. Archer continues that many 'ignore the amount of labor and thought required to transmute, not only the general tendency, but even a very special aptitude, into accomplished mastery' (Archer, 1888/1957).

One reason why the 'labor', 'thought' and skill that actually go into 'good' acting is often not recognized or acknowledged is that our dominant style of acting—psychological realism—strives to appear 'natural', effortless, thus giving the erroneous impression that it actually *is*. In the words of Lee Strasberg: '[i]t was the fact that it was not acting which made it great acting' (Hornby, 1992). And actors themselves have tended to downplay the craft, artistry and creativity that they bring to their work. Australian actor Bob Hornery, for example, believes that acting 'is something your common sense should tell you', a matter of simply working out where you 'will be standing on stage so that everyone can be seen and heard' (Trengrove, 1991). If only it were that easy.

There is also a prevalent belief that acting emanates from special qualities possessed by the actor: good looks, tenacity, presence, talent, sincerity, integrity, and so on. This misconception is perpetuated to a great extent by the film and TV industries' commodification of the actor as 'Personality', 'Celebrity', 'Star'. Interest in how actors create their roles is often limited to how they look. A great deal of media hype surrounded Nicole Kidman's donning a disfiguring prosthetic nose to play Virginia Woolf, or Charlize Theron daring to put on weight for her role in *Monster*. These superficial aspects of their characterisation received more press than their acting skills. It was as if that is all they had to do to play their parts. Nor is this restricted to the film industry. Reviews for Nicole Kidman's performance in *The Blue Room* took almost exclusive interest in her nude scene. An *Evening Standard* review says it all: 'No—repeat, no—cellulite' (Steyn, 1999).

1.3.2 Acting is Mimetic

'acting is imitative or it is nothing' (Archer, 1888/1957).

Yet another commonplace objection to acting being a creative art is that, being necessarily mimetic, it does not have the capacity for abstraction like other art forms, such as music or painting. According to Archer, acting 'stands at the very opposite pole from music, with sculpture, painting, poetry, in intermediate positions' (Archer, 1888/1957). The implication here is clear and damning: if actors only copy what is already out there, then they do not, *cannot*, create anything that is new or original.

But the truth of the matter is that acting is not merely mimetic. Actors do not simply mimic people they see out there in the 'real' world, however 'true to life' their portrayals might seem. In addition to insightful observation, actors use their imagination, intellect, artistic intuition and expressive skills to create their roles. In fact, Koestler points out that direct copies of nature are impossible, rather *all* artistic representation must 'pass through two distorting lenses: the artist's mind' and the 'medium of expression' (Koestler, 1970). In the words of Zola, one of Naturalism's most dedicated advocates: a work of art *'est un coin de la création vu à travers un tempérament'*—'a work of art is a corner of the world *seen through a medium'* (Zola, 1959). In other words, all art, even the most realistic, is abstracted. Plato was only too aware of this: it formed the basis of his objection to all art:

> The painter when he paints a bed, paints [...] a world of appearances, a debased version of what in nature is already only an appearance, since even the carpenter's solid wooden object is no more than a particular instance of the Idea *bed*, which alone can be said to be real and true (Barish, 1981).

1.3.3 Acting is Ephemeral

acting is 'forever carving a statue of snow' Lawrence Barrett (Cole & Chinoy, 1970).

Acting is ephemeral. The actor does not produce an artifact which can be hung on a wall, published, placed on a pedestal, and which has the capacity to live on and, like truly 'great' art—*masterpieces*—pass the test of time. George Henry Lewes, eminent nineteenth-century theatre critic, exclaims: the 'curtain falls—the artist is annihilated. Succeeding generations may be told of his genius; none can test it' (Lewes, 1875/1957). Given the logocentric tendency of the West, which has always privileged objects over acts, things over events, nouns over verbs, it is not surprising that the art object, the artifact, has been valued. It is a reason why, until the last thirty years, traditional university theatre and drama studies were restricted to the study of texts, not performance. A text is recoverable and analyzable, whereas performance is ephemeral, here and now, slippery, elusive, denying recovery and, putatively, defying analysis. It may be recorded, but then becomes a recording of the performance and not the performance itself.

Despite these difficulties, however, events and their sub-categories (acts, actions, performances and processes) are not so easily marginalized. Goethe's Faust was definitely on to something when he proclaimed: 'In the Beginning was the Act!' He makes the same philosophical case that certain Eastern philosophies have made for over two thousand years. In Buddhism, for example, *events* and not *things* are the 'fundamental components of universes' (George, 1999). To quote Garma Chang: 'things do not exist: only events' (Chang, 1971). In Sufi, Hindu and Taoist world views, the world 'cannot be understood as an assemblage of entities', but rather 'must be understood directly, as moving, interrelated events' (Melrose, 1989). In the West, the recognition of the event as the 'basic datum' was central to early twentieth-century Process philosophy. In *The Method of Extensive Abstraction*, Whitehead writes of 'event-particles' as the basic components of the universe, and proposes that 'the concept of an ether of events should be substituted for that of a material ether' (Whitehead, 1920). Since Whitehead, we have witnessed the emergence of Event philosophy as well as Quantum, Chaos and Complexity theories, which have all come to conceive of the event as primary. In the words of event philosophers Roberto Casati and Achille Varzi:

> One could take the massive indeterminacy [...] to be evidence that systematic theorizing about events is impossible. On the other hand, it is not clear that the indeterminacy is any worse in the case of events than in the case of objects, and we seem able to theorize in a systematic fashion about them (Casati & Varzi, 2006).

Natalie Crohn Schmitt observes that in science:

> it has come to be understood that the event is the unit of things real—that energy not matter, is the basic datum. In the increasingly widespread perception of reality as endless process, performance, not the art object, becomes primary (Crohn Schmitt, 1990).

Running parallel to this (re)cognition of events, reception theories have destabilized the determinacy and permanency of the aesthetic object, arguing that creative products only ever exist as such *in the event* of their reception. Roland Barthes, for example, relocates meaning/s in the instance of reception, where the text performs for its audience: 'there is no other time than that of the enunciation and every text is eternally written *here* and *now*' (Barthes, 1984).

So, to sum, the focus seems to be clear: we only need to peel away a few of the layers of prejudice and disturb a little of the historical dust, and the creativity of acting will be revealed. Except that one finds another obstacle obscuring the view. There remains one factor still undermining the creativity of acting, lurking where one least expected it. If anything has undermined the recognition of the actor's creativity it is none other than our commonly accepted, hegemonic definition of acting.

Acting is diminished by its own definition...

2 What is Acting?

'Acting' invokes many synonyms: 'playing', 'pretending', 'impersonating', 'imitating', 'performing', 'representing'—to cite just a few. It is a term which is used in two contexts: there is the acting that is commonplace behaviour, occurring in everyday life and there is the acting that is an art, craft or body of skills practised by actors in theatre, radio, film and television. It is frequently—and incorrectly—assumed that the latter 'naturally' evolves from the former. This misconception is, to a degree, understandable since to act in both its everyday and its theatrical senses have existed side-by-side since their first recorded uses. In its everyday sense 'to act' ('to bring into action, bring about, produce, perform, work, make, do') was first cited in 1594 ('Act' *v* Def. 2). This was the same year it was used in a theatrical sense: 'carry out or represent in mimic action (an ideal, incident, or story; to perform a play)' ('Act' *v* Def.4). Undoubtedly, they are related, but it is misleading to consider them synonymous.

Ostensibly, acting as a craft or art is easily identified—we know it when we see it—but when it comes to definitions the term proves to be surprisingly slippery. Attempts to formulate a definition have been frustrated by the fact that there is no *one* acting, but *multiple* 'actings' or acting styles. Despite the current hegemony of psychological realism, Western acting praxis is today, as it has been historically, multifarious. There has never been one, universal acting style in the West. Meyerhold, Brecht, Artaud and Grotowski, for instance, all proposed a different acting for their theatres, and in the contemporary context, Robert Wilson's acting—slick, precise, virtuoso—is very different to the seeming anti-virtuosity of Forced Entertainment or the jarring bricolage of styles evident in the Wooster Group. But even though acting has been various and multivalent, it is generally accepted that common to all styles is one irreducible factor: *impersonation*. In *Actors on Acting*, Cole and Chinoy make the point: 'impersonation or the assumption of dramatic personality' is a prerequisite of all acting (Cole & Chinoy, 1970).

However, as there are many acting styles, there are also multiple types of impersonation in Western theatre traditions. A heuristic continuum can be formulated with the 'actor-as-abstract' at one extreme, the 'actor-as-self' at the other, and significant coordinates along the axis:

Abstract—-Type—-Individuated   Type—-Highly   Individuated   Character—-Multiple Personae—-Self

1. *Actor-as-abstract*:

Actor is 'objectified' or represents 'one of the formal elements of a production', as in the works of Robert Wilson (Bishop, 1988). Other examples include: Maurice Maeterlinck's actor-as-puppet, Gordon Craig's Über-marionette, Oskar Schlemmer's Tänzermensch, Tadeusz Kantor's mannequin.

---

2. *Actor-as-type*:

Actor impersonates a conventional type or stock character. Examples can be found in *commedia dell'arte,* melodrama, pantomime.

3. *Actor-as-individuated type*:

Actor takes as basis for impersonation a social, historical, cultural or theatrical type and incorporates individual traits. Medieval Mystery plays, Restoration comedies, farce, and the theatre of Brecht provide examples of this.

4. *Actor-as-highly-individuated character*:

Actor's impersonation (re)presents a psychologically complex and motivated character. This is exemplified in Naturalism and its associated acting style psychological realism.

5. *Actor-as-multiple-personae*:

Actor's impersonation is comprised of multiple identities, a bricolage of personae. This composite might include various manifestations of the character and, possibly, the actor's 'self'. On playing John Proctor in *LSD (...Just the High Points...),* Willem Dafoe claims that he 'makes no distinction between being himself in the first part, playing John Proctor in the second, and playing himself (stoned) rehearsing John Proctor in the third' (Auslander, 1985).

6. *Actor-as-'self'*:

Associated with performance art and postmodern performance where the acting, to borrow Michael Kirby's term, is 'non-matrixed': the actor 'never behaves as if he were anyone other than himself. He never represents elements of character. He merely carries out certain actions' (Kirby, 2002).

Despite the existence of these different types of impersonation in the West, psychological realism dominates. In fact, in most current definitions, impersonation is conflated with the representation of a psychologically complex and highly individuated character. Acting is fundamentally:
- 'the art or practice of representing a *character* in a dramatic production' (*The Penguin English Dictionary*);
- 'the performing art in which an actor by means of movement, gesture and intonation attempts to realize a fictional *character* for the stage, for motion picture, and for television' (*The New Encyclopaedia Britannica*);
- 'the representation of a usually fictional *character* on stage or in films' (*Columbia Encyclopedia*).

Put simply, acting = characterisation. In the words of Peter Thomson: we 'now take it for granted that the relationship of actor to character is at the heart of the theatrical enterprise' (Thomson, 2000).

Well, isn't it?

While we may find it difficult—almost impossible—not to view acting through the prism of character, character did not always occupy centre-stage, nor did it exhaust the actor's creative skills. It is timely to recall the etymology of acting: from the Latin *actuary,* 'acting' means a 'thing done': the actor is 'one who does things' (Zarrilli, 2002). William Worthen reinforces the point: 'to act is simply to do something, to express or create meaning through action (Greek: *drama*: an 'act' or 'deed)' (Worthen, 1984). However, over the last century and into the present, the *doing* has been increasingly sidelined, and *character* has assumed a privileged position. Acting has become primarily about character creation, marking a shift from *doing* to *being,* a pre-occupation with the embodiment of *subjects* over engaging in *actions.*

Yet it is important to remind ourselves that *character* has not always been foremost in acting because, quite simply, *character* itself is a modern concept. Thomson makes this point by way of anecdote: a 'successful young director (Jude Kelly) asked John Barton to define his attitude to character in Shakespeare's plays'. Barton replied that Shakespeare: 'would have associated the word 'character' with the formation of letters in writing or printing, not with invented creatures, not with people at all' (Thomson, 2000). Barton is not entirely accurate here: in Shakespeare's time 'character' was applied to a person's physical features, particularly in how they reflected their moral character ('Character' Def. 10): 'thou hast a mind that suits with this thy fair and outward character' (*Twelfth Night* 1. ii. 51). In the theatrical sense, however, 'character' was not used until the mid-seventeenth century: '[a] personality invested with distinctive attributes and qualities, by a novelist or dramatist; also, the personality or 'part' assumed by an actor' (*OED* 'Character' Def. 17.a). *Impersonation* in the sense of 'the dramatic representation of character' did not enter English until the early nineteenth century (*OED* 'Impersonation' Def. 2) and although its etymological predecessor *personation* was in use at the end of the sixteenth century, it did not mean characterisation. Edward Burns makes the point that on the Elizabethan stage to 'personate is to use the resources of one's person to present, not another being in the Stanislavskian sense [i.e. in the modern sense] but a thing done, action in this sense' (Burns, 1990). Moving forward in time, *characterisation* was not the object for eighteenth-century actors either. As Joseph Roach details in his excellent book *The Player's Passion: studies in the science of acting,* playing the passions was at the heart of acting—and, moreover, was what delighted audiences.

One must, then, be wary of the modern tendency to insert character where it has no place. This came home to me when I was recently re-reading *Paradoxe sur le Comédien* (*The Paradox of Acting*). A watershed work in acting theory, it has set the parameters of a debate which has been ongoing. Lee Strasberg claims that any 'discussion' of acting almost invariably touches on Diderot's famous paradox: to move the audience the actor must himself remain unmoved' (Strasberg, 1957). While the paradox is, indeed, very intriguing, it is not my primary concern here—rather, it is how *character* has crept into English translations of *Paradoxe sur le Comédien*. Take, for instance, the following excerpt from Walter Herries Pollock's late-nineteenth century, definitive English translation:

> All the emotions he has given to you. The actor is tired, you are unhappy; he has had exertion without feeling, you feeling without exertion. Were it otherwise the player's lot would be the most wretched on earth: but he is not the *person* he represents [my emphasis] (Diderot, 1830/1957).

In the original, however, Diderot writes: '*mais il n'est pas le personnage*' (Diderot, 1830/1922). Pollock has substituted 'person' for '*personnage*', which may seem reasonable enough, except that for Diderot, *personnage* did not describe a 'person' (or, as is suggested here, 'character'). Consistent with common usage in his time, Diderot used *personnage* to denote certain moral and physical qualities extrapolated from an historical or eminent figure, the text, and from the actor's own imagination, and which the actor imitates. It is understandable how definitional slippage has at times occurred and the assumption made that Diderot must have been referring to character as we now use the term. For example, when he writes of the 'character that you have to render'—'*le caractère que tu avais à rendre*'—it could be assumed as meaning 'theatrical character', but in keeping with its usage at the time, it would most certainly have referred here to a person's moral disposition and not the person or character per se. It is vital to recognize that in Diderot's time the French *caractère* and English 'character' stood for the moral qualities, multiple strands, as it were, which had not yet been woven into the integrated, singular personality or subject of our modern conception. The notion of character as a person or subject was to come later, in the mid-eighteenth century. However, even then, it is still not our modern theatrical sense of the word: rather, character remains an abstraction, an hypostatization, a metonym for moral actions: '*[i]l désigne en particulier la manière d'être moral d'ou, par métonymie, les personnes envisagés sous l'angle de leur personnalité*' ('caractère', 1992). It was the same in English: 'person regarded in the abstract as the possessor of specified qualities' (*OED* 'Character' Def. 16a). The 'person' is only, if ever, envisaged through the moral traits he or she displays: they are primary. On the few occasions in *Paradoxe* where *caractère* does seem to denote the individual 'person', it in fact implies a 'type': '*toutes sortes de caractères*' or '*caractères divers*'. 'Types', which are more akin to Aristotle's concept of 'types of *natural dispositions*' that are 'drawn along the lines of the universal, not the individual' (Else, 1957).

Yet, character is so ingrained that it is difficult for us to conceive of acting without it at the centre. So, what happened? When and why did character assume centre stage—and how does the rise of character impact on how we think about the creativity of acting?

2.1 Emergence and Rise of Character

'*it is the character that is the starting point of everything*' Constant Coquelin (Cole & Chinoy, 1970).

It is clear that, towards the end of the nineteenth century, acting was radically redefined first and foremost as *characterisation*. This trend toward a character-centric acting had been gradual. The eighteenth century preoccupation with the actor's skilful rendering of the passions remained significant in acting and its theories. William Archer, for example, claims that reproducing the physical effects of the so-called simple emotions 'must be the very groundwork of the actor's art' (Archer, 1888/1957). And by describing acting as the playing of passions, Tommaso Salvini (1829-1915), the greatly applauded actor of the nineteenth century, would not have been out of place on the eighteenth-century stage:

> I felt the need of studying, not books alone, but men and things. [...] In short, all the passions for good and evil which have a root in human nature. I needed to study out the manner of rendering these passions (Cole & Chinoy, 1970).

Salvini goes on, however, to describe a process which did not concern the eighteenth-century actor:

> I must become capable of *identifying myself with one or another personage* to such an extent as to lead the audience into the illusion that the real personage, and not a copy, is before them [my emphasis] (Cole & Chinoy, 1970).

Over the course of the nineteenth century, the playing of the passions became subordinated to realizing character. George Henry Lewes claims that the actor should not merely present the emotions, but more specifically, 'the emotions of the character he is personating [...] the integrity of which is never sacrificed to isolated effects' (Lewes, 1875/1957). This is a crucial change. Whereas for Diderot the meticulous scoring of a *rôle* gave a performance cohesion and unity, now it relies on the 'integrity' or unity of a character. In the highly influential *On Actors and the Art of Acting* (1878), Lewes stresses this point: William Charles Macready, for example, lacked 'that sympathy with the character which would have given an impressive unity to his performance—it was a 'thing of threads and patches,' not a whole'. Charles Mathews, on the other hand, is commended for 'a certain artistic power of preserving the unity of character'. Moreover, what is clearly spelled out now is how this 'unity of character' is to be achieved: 'sympathy with the character'. This is the paradigmatic shift (one which occurred well before Stanislavsky turned it into a System): successful acting now relies on how closely actors sympathize and identify with their characters. Lewes praises the actress Eliza Felix Rachel for the way 'she thoroughly identified herself with the character'. Macready is redeemed by a performance in which he 'did not stand outside the character', but rather, 'felt himself to be the person, and having identified himself with the character' expressed 'what the character felt'. Although in *Masks or Faces?*, Archer does not subscribe to the possibility of total identification or transformation into character, he still uses the new terminology: *'incarnate in your personage'*, *'work myself into a character'*, *'putting on the character'*, *'entering into the skin of Tartuffe'*, *'to live in it'*.

Searching for the factors behind this stellar rise of character, one finds three major influences:

2.1.1 Romantic Dramatic Theory

'between classicism and romanticism was a shift in general focus from plot to character' (Carlson, 1984).

In *Theories of the Theatre*, Marvin Carlson observes that English critics such as William Hazlitt (1788-1830) and the German Romantics shared 'an interest in character rather than actions as the central element of drama'. This trend toward privileging character was especially prevalent in the theorizing of Greek tragedy. Aristotle had not held the tragic hero or character (*éthos*) to be primary, but rather action (*praxis*). Elizabeth Belfiore (1992), Gerald Else (1957) and John Jones (1971) have conducted thorough re-readings of Aristotle's *Poetics,* to reveal 'that we have imported the tragic hero into the *Poetics* where the concept has no place' (Jones, 1971). The nineteenth-century Romantic theorists not only inserted the tragic hero where he or she never existed, but also focused on 'those parts of the *Poetics* which seemed to promise human and psychological interest' (Jones, 1971). Jones notes that Aristotle never mentions the tragic hero in the *Poetics* and, in fact, insists 'that Tragedy does not imitate human beings'. He quotes Aristotle: '[t]ragedy is an imitation not of human beings but of action and life' (*Poetics* 50a16). According to Belfiore, *éthos* never meant dramatic character in the *Poetics*, but was used to indicate either 'what kind of choice is made by an agent of a dramatic action' or 'as one of the six qualitative parts of a tragedy, second in importance to plot' (Belfiore, 1992).

Shakespeare is not exempt from this trend of prioritizing character. Indeed, it is by reference to Shakespeare that one can most readily trace how potent character became. Hazlitt, for example, views Shakespeare's major strength as his characterisation: in his view, Shakespeare was distinguished from his peers by his ability to create characters who were each 'as much itself, and as absolutely independent of the rest, as if they were living persons, not fictions of the mind' (Carlson, 1984). In fact, it would have been impossible for Shakespeare to think of character in this modern sense. Instead, as Burns claims, the Elizabethan character is best described in terms of 'pictures produced in action only momentarily', a claim supported, he argues, by the commonplace of devices such as 'allegorical vignettes', 'meta-theatrical presentations', disguise and cross-dressing (Burns, 1990). It might, in fact, be more accurate to view the Shakespearean character as discontinuous, a body of multiple, often conflicting dispositions—and ultimately determined by circumstances and events. Where the action goes, or needs to go, the character follows: the best way Rosalind can escape her uncle's court, survive in the world, and woo Orlando is to assume a male guise. Macbeth is explicit: 'Strange things I have in head, that will to hand;/ Which must be acted ere they may be scann'd' (*Macbeth* 3.iv. 138-39).

However, in the nineteenth century, the order is reversed: character becomes primary, the source of and key to action. Such characters even burst their fictional boundaries. In our contemporary context, the idea that characters can *exist* beyond the events of the play does not seem extraordinary; to ask the actor playing the part how many children has Lady Macbeth, for example, may seem entirely reasonable— but at the end of the nineteenth century, and even well into the twentieth, this was revolutionary. For the first time, it was presumed that 'each dramatic persona has life anterior and (if he survives the disease of the fifth act) posterior to the text' (Roach, 1985). Character biographies became not just of interest to the actors playing the part, but to the public. The popularity of works such as Mary Cowden Clarke's *The Girlhood of Shakespeare's Heroines* (1851-52) is evidence of this.

And if Romantic dramatic theory served to promote character to new heights, then the emerging aesthetic of Naturalism ensured that the task was completed.

2.1.2 Naturalism

'*a man of flesh and bones on the stage, taken from reality, scientifically analyzed, without one lie*' Émile Zola (Cole & Chinoy, 1970).

Zola's 'man of flesh and bones' was at the centre of the theatre of Naturalism. Otto Brahm, Naturalism's major exponent in Germany, is unequivocal: '[w]e no longer wish merely to play 'effective scenes' but rather wish to present complete characters with the whole conglomerate of qualities with which they are endowed' (Cole & Chinoy, 1970). The agenda is articulated succinctly by Strindberg in his preface to *Miss Julie*. Here he outlines—from text to make-up—Naturalism's mission. Particularly noteworthy is the significance he places on character: most of the preface is, in fact, concerned with the question of character. Strindberg argues for a new concept of character for the stage—a character that does not represent 'an individual who has stopped developing, or who has moulded himself to a fixed role in life' (Strindberg, 1888/1976). In contrast to this, the new drama of Naturalism, according to Strindberg, must contain characters that mirror 'how richly complex a human soul is'. To highlight this complexity, Strindberg plumbs the depths of the play's characters. No rock unturned, he lists, for example, 'the many possible motivations for *Miss Julie*'s unhappy fate':

> The passionate character of her mother; the upbringing misguidedly inflicted on her by her father; her own character; and the suggestive effect of her fiancé upon her weak and degenerate brain. Also, more immediately, the festive atmosphere of Midsummer Night; her father's absence; her menstruation; her association with animals; the intoxicating effect of the dance; the midsummer twilight; the powerfully aphrodisiac influence of the flowers; and finally, the chance that drove these two people together into a private room—plus of course the passion of the sexually inflamed man (Strindberg, 1888/1976).

And in the case of Jean, not content to stop at the present, Strindberg predicts his future:

> So he survives the battle unharmed, and will quite possibly end as an *hotelier*; and even if he does not become a Rumanian [*sic!*] count, his son will probably get to university and very likely end up on the bench (Strindberg, 1888/1976).

In comparison, plot is given short shrift, just one paragraph, and even then it is subordinated to character. Strindberg claims that he has kept the plot of *Miss Julie* simple because:

> I believe that what most interests people today is the psychological process. Our prying minds are not content merely with seeing something happen—they must know why it happens (Strindberg, 1888/1976).

In the words of John Galsworthy (1867-1933): 'a human being is the best plot there is' (Carlson, 1984).

This 'human being', the individual subject of everyday life and prototype for the new character of Naturalism, was itself a new conception—the product of emerging philosophical and scientific theories of the human body/mind which came under the disciplinary umbrella of Psychology.

2.1.3 The Psychological Character

'a network of endowments and limitations, themselves the complex product of heredity and environment' (Roach, 1985).

One should caution against conceiving of Psychology as a cohesive discourse, defined by a single set of theories, research methods, let alone agendas. Historically, it was more accurately a wide-ranging field of investigations conducted by individuals. The scope was broad: from Wilhelm Wundt's enterprise to establish a scientific, experimental psychology to Sigmund Freud's theories of the unconscious mind; Hermann Ebbinghaus's investigations on memory to Ivan Pavlov's work on conditioned reflexes. Yet despite this, common to all the research and its theories was a preoccupation with the individual and an assumption of its primacy. Burns makes the point that with the advent of modern Psychology in the nineteenth century 'forces and effects' previously conceived as 'impersonal' or 'interpersonal', become 'personal'—located in the mental states and processes of the individual (Burns, 1990). In a radical shift, the inner-world of the individual is prioritized and postulated as the source of and motivation for action. Raymond Williams observes that *psychology* and *psychological* assume the existence of:

> a separable or at least radically distinguishable *inner world*, within which processes of feeling and relationship and activity can be described 'in their own terms', such processes often being taken as primary, with the *outside world—nature or society*—seen as secondary or contingent (Williams, 1976).

It is in this context that the actor William Charles Macready can redefine the player's art:

> To fathom the depths of character, to trace its latent motives, to feel its finest quiverings of emotion, to comprehend the thoughts that are hidden under words, and thus possess one's self of the actual mind of the individual man (Cole & Chinoy, 1970).

Inner motivations and hereditary factors are now seen as crucial to the shaping of the individual and the theatrical character. It is the subterranean world—the psychology of the character—which now becomes central both to the definition of acting and its creativity.

This new product of acting—the psychological character—required both a new acting and new theories of acting. Initially, the new directors attempted to resolve the problem pragmatically. In order to support the illusion of characters behaving naturally, actors should appear as if they are not actually acting. André Antoine, therefore, used with rare exception in his *Théâtre-Libre* productions amateur actors, who were not 'contaminated' by traditional actor training. Brahm, in a similar vein, called for 'human beings who find the emotions of the character to be represented from within and who express these with a simple natural voice' and without regard to the conventional gestures of 'stock types' (Cole & Chinoy, 1970). Any hint of the *theatrical* should be underplayed or, even, eliminated. One radical way was to *ignore* the audience: one of the most controversial practices of the late nineteenth century was 'Antoine's Back', named after the common practice at the *Théâtre-Libre* of actors turning their backs on the audience. It caused quite a stir. In the words of Zola: this 'doesn't seem like much, but it is enormous for us in France' (Carlson, 1984).

This denial of the presence of the audience was, in turn, further enabled by technological innovations, namely the introduction of gas lighting and limelight. While the 'intensity of limelight' virtually blinded actors, cutting them off from the audience, gas lighting in the auditorium could be dimmed, further obscuring the audience, and relegating them to the role of voyeurs (Mackintosh, 1993). These acting conventions and technical innovations all contributed to the enterprise of Naturalism, putatively convincing the audience that they were witnessing *real* people on the stage.

In practice, however, these new acting conventions were not always deemed successful. As an audience member, Lewes, for example, found 'Antoine's Back' untenable:

> French actors, when not excellent, carry the reaction too far; and in the attempt to be natural forget the *optique du théâtre*, and the demands of art. They will sit upon side sofas, and speak with their faces turned away from the audiences, so that half their words are lost (Lewes, 1875/1957).

But, while Lewes may have been disturbed by the extremes of this so-called *natural* acting, he was an integral part of the push for a new *character-centric* acting. Rather than merely impose a new set of theatrical conventions, Lewes and others realized that more fundamental changes were required.

2.2 Being a Creative Actor

The conventional artist 'cannot be the part, but he tries to act it' (Lewes, 1875/1957).

Among the nineteenth-century English theorists of theatre and acting, Lewes stands out. William Archer credited him as being the 'the most highly trained thinker who ever applied himself to the study of theatrical art in England' (Roach, 1985), and George Bernard Shaw is hyperbolic in his praise of Lewes as: 'the most able and brilliant critic between Hazlitt and our own contemporaries' (Carlson, 1984). Lewes had also been an actor, but it is for *On Actors and the Art of Acting* that he is primarily known. In the main, this work is a critical investigation of a number of eminent nineteenth-century English and European actors: Edmund Kean, Charles Kean, Eliza Felix Rachel, William Charles Macready, William Farren, Charles Mathews, Frédéric Lemaître, Mr and Mrs Keeley and Tommaso Salvini to name the most prominent. At a first glance, it may appear as superficial musings on acting by a Victorian theatre-enthusiast, but *On Actors and the Art of Acting* deserves a more attentive reading because it clearly articulates criteria for what came to be considered *creative* acting:

> the success of the personation will depend upon the vividness of the actor's sympathy, and his honest reliance on the truth of his own *individual expression*, in preference to the conventional expressions which may be accepted on the stage. *This is the great actor, the creative artist* [my emphasis] (Lewes, 1875/1957).

Lewes defines 'personation' as speaking 'through the *persona* or character'; when the actor 'for the moment is what he *represents*'. This marks a modern use of the word, distinct from its earlier uses which, as we have seen, are associated with the embodiment of actions. Lewes then proceeds to identify what theorists and practitioners increasingly perceived as the major obstacle to this new, creative acting: the conventional, codified practices inherited from the previous century:

> The majority have not learned to speak, much less to act; they mouth and gabble, look at the audience instead of their interlocutors, fling emphasis at random, mistake violence for emotion, grimace for humor, and express their feelings by signs as conventional and unlike nature as the gestures of a ballet-dancer. *Good acting, on the contrary, like good writing, is remarkable for its individuality. It charms by its truth; and the truth is always original* [my emphasis] (Lewes, 1875/1957).

This 'old' acting will no longer suffice; it is far too generalized and broad, not refined enough to realize the new characters of Naturalism, with all their complexities and idiosyncrasies: 'in modern drama we demand,' writes Lewes, 'the minute individualities of character'—a shift 'from the simple and general to the complex and individual'. In place, therefore, of conventional forms of expression, actors must draw upon their own 'inner' resources to create their own 'individual expression'. The actress Rachel epitomizes for Lewes this new hallmark of the actor's creativity:

> Rachel *personated*, she spoke through the character, she suffered her inward feelings to express themselves in outward signs; she had not to cast about her for the outward signs which conventionally expressed such feelings. [...] Those few she personated, those she *created* [my emphasis] (Lewes, 1875/1957).

However, acting which depended on the actor's own original expression was not without its problems. It raised a number of intriguing questions for the theorist and, no doubt, pressing problems for the actor: *'How do I find the appropriate expression? By what standards will my own unique expression be measured? Will my audience 'get' my meaning?'* Answers to these questions had to be found.

Directorial supervision was clearly one solution, and actors did increasingly rely on directors, who could tell them if their intentions were clearly manifested. Another obvious solution would be for actors to maintain an aesthetic distance so they could monitor their own acting. Actors had, after all, always done this to a greater or lesser extent. However, now this kind of distancing becomes problematic. The new ideal of acting, whereby actors identify with their characters, renders any aesthetic distance, any gap between actor and character undesirable. The ultimate solution for the problem of finding the appropriate expression was not to be found in encouraging gaps but, in fact, in the opposite: the actor's total identification with the character. Lewes suggests that if the actor 'personates', or 'is what he represents', then like the great Rachel, the appropriate feelings will express themselves. In short: it is believed that if the actor can thoroughly identify with the character, then all else will *naturally* follow. Coquelin writes:

> If you have assimilated the essence of your personage, his exterior will follow quite naturally, and if there is any picturesqueness, it will come of itself. It is the mind which constructs the body (Cole & Chinoy, 1970).

This movement toward individual expression marks a radical shift: what is *natural*, *genuine* and *original* is privileged—and *acting*, with its basis in convention, pretense and imitation, is made pejorative. It is not surprising, therefore, that Lewes should end up promoting *being* over *acting*. The conventional artist:

> cannot *be* the part, but he tries to *act* it, and is thus necessarily driven to adopt those conventional means of expression with which the traditions of the stage abound. Instead of allowing a strong feeling to express itself through its natural signs, he seizes upon the conventional signs, either because in truth there is no strong feeling moving him, or because he is not artist enough to give it genuine expression (Lewes, 1875/1957).

Toward the end of the nineteenth century, *being* is the new ideal, one that has persisted, to varying degrees, in contemporary psychological realism. Lee Strasberg maintained that if 'you want to be an actor, don't *act*. *Be*' (Hornby, 1992). For actors to *be*, they must penetrate their own *inner* selves and assimilate the *essence* of their characters. Thus, acting becomes both *character*-centric and *actor*-centric, a double shift of focus which in turn, necessitates a completely new creative process.

Firstly, according to Coquelin, the actor 'must read the play carefully over many times, until he has grasped the intention of the author and the meaning of the character he is to represent' (Cole & Chinoy, 1970). Actors have, of course, always studied their roles. Diderot, for example, praised the actress Clairon for doing precisely that. Her genius lay, according to Diderot, in her ability to choose a *modèle idéal* and score a *rôle*. The difference now is that, for the first time, the actor is called upon to make a psychological study of the text and his or her character. To recall Macready: to 'fathom the depths of character', 'trace its latent motives' and 'comprehend the thoughts that are hidden under words'.

Secondly, and crucially, the *actor* must identify with his or her *character*. This was the most important question that the nineteenth-century theorists and actors had to confront: 'how the interior life of the character and the interior life of the actor could somehow be brought together' (Roach, 1985). This was perceived as primarily a psychological problem, and if Psychology posed the problem, then it also provided the answers. Taking their lead from Psychology, acting theorists and critics made the assumption that inner processes are primary and affective. One of the most fundamental premises of psychology is that emotional reflexes and impulses proceed 'from interior to exterior, from subjective to objective: a psychic tremor stirs a physical act' (Roach, 1985). Acting theory and practice assumed that this flow from inner to outer could be profitably harnessed: through careful study and concentration, the appropriate feelings or thoughts could be induced, and it would then follow that the actor would produce quite naturally the *right* expression. To this end, Archer borrowed the concept of *autosuggestion* from Eduard von Hartmann's influential *Philosophy of the Unconscious* (1868), adopting the term to describe the 'mental concentration' that some actors utilize in helping them 'get into their character' (Archer, 1888/1957). Actor Wilson Barrett described this process to Archer:

> I always endeavour to get a short time to myself, in my dressing room, to think over my character and work myself into it. [...] I have noticed the same thing in other actors (Archer, 1888/1957).

Autosuggestion is counter-balanced by the somatic process of *innervation*, which Archer derived from Charles Darwin's *The Expression of Emotions in Man and Animals* (1872). Archer uses the term innervation to describe Macready's practice of shaking a ladder offstage to achieve a required level of rage. In other words, a physical action, and not a mental frame of mind, is used to bring about the desired affect. Despite acknowledging its occurrence, Archer concludes that as 'a rule, however, mental concentration, rather than any physical device, is resorted to in order to overcome the difficulty of "striking twelve at once"' (Archer, 1888/1957).

A psychological working 'into' the character is never enough in itself: the actor has to produce the goods. Archer himself acknowledged that 'emotion alone, without the faculty of dramatic expression, will not make itself felt across the footlights'. Lewes wrote in a similar vein that it 'matters little what the actor *feels;* what he can *express* gives him distinctive value'. However, in the acting of psychological realism, an assumption of 'inner' to 'outer' is evident and prevalent to this day: Australian actor Bud Tingwell comments:

> The most important thing I learnt was that if you understood the play to the point where you could *think* the thought processes of a character, everything would slot into place. [...] If you get inside the thought processes something else *does* take over. If your thinking is right then you shouldn't need to worry (Trengrove, 1991).

Another concept that acting borrowed from psychology was the *subconscious*. It would have been hard for acting theorists not to. Roach comments that by 'the 1870s the word *unconscious* and its physiological counterpart *subconscious* achieved popularity pervasive enough to constitute a fashion' (Roach, 1985). This newly conceived *subconscious* came to be perceived as the wellspring of the actor's creativity: the treasure trove which the actor only needed to unlock to be truly *creative*. The capability, however, to plumb one's inner creative source was not universal. There were some fortunate actors who possessed the right temperament, or in modern parlance, 'psychological make-up', to afford them easy access. Nineteenth-century actor Mr Bancroft acknowledges with some awe that Mrs Bancroft possessed 'nerves and muscles [which] sensitively respond to the touch' of her creative imagination (Archer,

1888/1957). For those less fortunate, assistance was required. It became necessary, therefore, to provide theories which would explain how the actor could tap into their inner source of creativity and coax it out. This, of course, would become, in no small part, Stanislavsky's mission.

The monumental shift that took place in nineteenth-century acting, and continues to resonate today, was that it became in no small part—and fundamentally—a psychological process, an 'inner' process, eluding, at times, even the actors themselves. Archer comments that he 'could not reasonably expect' his 'obliging informants to study a disquisition on psychology' or 'to be accurately introspective of their experiences'. Describing himself as 'an amateur psychologist', Archer looked forward to a time when 'a better-equipped psychology may thread the maze [of mimetic emotion] to its innermost recesses'. It is apposite to recall that the full title of his work is *Masks or Faces? A Study in the Psychology of Acting*. It should also be noted that, beyond his theatre credentials, Lewes was also the author of *The Problems of Life and Mind* (1878). Although incomplete at his death, it was acclaimed for its penetration of, among other things, psychological issues. Lewes was, therefore, part of the emerging science of Psychology, whose influence on acting was so significant. Woe betides the actor who ignores 'the psychological conditions on which effects depend' for, in Lewes' view, he or she will 'pass into the artificial' (Lewes, 1875/1957).

Thus, towards the end of the nineteenth century, two emerging strands started to converge: acting moved toward the embodiment of a unique individual, and psychology moved towards subject-positions as the source of creativity. The weaving together of these strands would serve to reinforce the emerging character-centric acting and, in turn, would have enduring implications for the creativity of acting.

This is the trend which Stanislavsky inherited, followed and turned into what remains not only the hegemonic theory of stage acting in the West, but also the standard account of its creativity.

3 Stanislavsky: Guru and Villain

I have a great respect for Stanislavsky—for his insights into acting and for the techniques and approaches he devised. Years after my Stanislavsky-based training, I continue to use aspects of his Psycho-Technique, Method of Physical Actions and Active Analysis in both my acting and teaching. However, you can and probably should be critical of those you admire—and when it comes to the creativity of acting, Stanislavsky is both guru *and* villain.

It would be difficult to overlook how often Stanislavsky invokes the actor's creativeness. No other acting theorist or practitioner before or since has invoked 'creativeness' and 'creative' so frequently, or was so preoccupied with identifying the creativity of acting. Stanislavsky himself commented that his 'lifelong concern has been how to get ever closer to the so-called 'System', that is to get ever closer to the nature of creativity' (Carnicke, 2000). In *My Life in Art*, he asks whether 'there can be no system for the creation of inspiration or system for creation itself?'. The question is, of course, rhetorical: for Stanislavsky, there could be such a 'system'—*a system for creative acting*. Stanislavsky's need for such a system was not merely theoretical, but practical and pressing. According to Tortsov, Stanislavsky's alter ego in *An Actor Prepares*, the theatres were brimming with examples of bad acting: derivative, imitative, clichéd and mechanical. In order to rescue the art of acting and enable actors to lay claims to being *true artists*, it was imperative for Stanislavsky that they identify and acknowledge their creativity. In *My Life in Art,* he writes: '[c]raftsmanship teaches the actor how to walk on the stage and play', but 'true art must teach him how to awaken consciously his subconscious creative self for its superconscious organic creativeness'.

In his exhortations for a new, creative acting, one that would arouse the actor's 'subconscious creative self', Stanislavsky was not saying anything particularly new. As discussed in the previous chapter, Victorian theatre critic and theorist George Henry Lewes had already observed that 'good' actors draw upon their own 'inner' resources. Nor was Stanislavsky rocking any boats when he claims in *An Actor Prepares* that 'the fundamental aim of our art is the creation of this inner life of a human spirit and its expression in artistic form' and the actor 'must fit his own human qualities to the life of this other person, and pour into it all of his own soul'. The acting these statements gesture toward had already emerged in the nascent theories of nineteenth-century acting critics and commentators such as Lewes.

However, Stanislavsky did push the envelope. If late-nineteenth century actors had only just been called upon to identify with their characters, Stanislavsky asks them to go further: to bring together the inner lives of their characters and their own inner selves to the point where they are frequently conceived as indivisible. In *Creating a Role* he writes:

> a great deal that is in your part and a great deal that is in you have become so intertwined that you cannot easily distinguish where the actor begins or the character ends. When you are in that state you come closer and closer to your part, you feel it inside you and feel yourself inside it (Stanislavski, 1961).

To 'feel *yourself* inside it': this is the radical shift, marking a new ideal for the actor—to get 'closer to the source of his inner life, his own nature as an actor, closer to that mysterious and intimate center which is the 'I' in a role' (Stanislavski, 1961). William Worthen makes the point that for Stanislavsky the 'committed and creative actor achieves an authentic sense of being through acting, the sense of 'I am' (Worthen, 1984). At this juncture, creativity and commitment come together in a fusion of *self-discovery* with its counterpart—*self-revelation*. In order to show that they have contacted the 'source' of their 'inner lives', actors must give the impression of self-revelation, creating the illusion of deeply felt sincerity and naturalness.

The progression is clear: while eighteenth-century acting can be defined as the skilful playing of the passions, and nineteenth-century acting the convincing portrayal of character, Stanislavsky gestures towards an acting which is revolutionary: *acting as self-revelation*. Lewes had already prioritized the actor's individual self-expression, but Stanislavsky takes it one step further: through the prism of character, 'true', 'creative' actors reveal their own 'essential' beings. In *Building a Character*, Stanislavsky observes:

> characterisation is the mask which hides the actor-individual. Protected by it he can bare his soul down to the last intimate detail. This is an important attribute or feature of characterisation (Stanislavski, 1977).

Given the times in which Stanislavsky practised and theorized, it is not difficult to understand why he would seek to promulgate a conception of acting as self-revelation: Naturalism emphasized 'real-life' depth and complexity of character and the Romantic ideal saw art as reflections of the soul. Worthen makes this point, noting that with a new emphasis on 'the powerful representation of dramatic character', acting moved closer to the ideals of Romanticism and Naturalism, but what pushed it over the line is the notion that it is somehow 'a dignified expression of the artist's identity' (Worthen, 1984).

Whatever Stanislavsky's reasons, this is our inheritance in the West: acting, *as an art*, is part *character-creation* and part *self-revelation*. The question of ratio is to this day a point of contention for theorists, intrigue for audiences and of practical concern for actors.

It is this concern that Stanislavsky's System aimed to address—and, in the process, achieve the radical: reveal a (*the*) blueprint of creative acting. If the most pressing issue confronting nineteenth-century acting theorists was to explain how the inner lives of actors and their characters could coalesce, then Stanislavsky showed how it was to be done. Stanislavsky established a methodology of unprecedented comprehensiveness for the actor's creative process, and although he was himself loathe to describe his System as definitive, aspects of it, particularly his psycho-technique, took root and continue to inform actors' creative processes. Had he just theorized, he may have receded into the shadows of theatre history, being of academic interest only, but his System—a detailed approach to acting by a respected actor with an insider's intimate knowledge—ensured his far-reaching attraction and influence. This is the reason Stanislavsky stands out, why Stan is guru for some.

3.1 Stanislavsky: Redefining the Actor's Creativity

But there is a flip side. Stanislavsky can also be cast as villain. As much as he extolled and promoted the creativity of acting, he simultaneously restricted the actor's authority and creativity in decisive ways.

Although it was not his main aim (and, therefore, often goes undetected), Stanislavsky defined not only the creative role of the *actor* but also what he saw as the other two major artists of the theatre: the *writer* and, more significantly, the *director*. If all their creative responsibilities were clearly defined and assigned, if each knew his or her place, this would facilitate, according to Stanislavsky in *My Life in Art*, the creation of a unified, well-integrated theatrical production:

> What is important to me is that the collective creation of all the artists of the stage be whole and complete and all those who helped to make the performance might serve for the same creative goal and bring their creations to one common denominator (Stanislavsky, 1924/1952).

In Stanislavsky's ideal collaboration, the playwright produces the seminal work and it is the duty of the actor and director to bring this to fruition:

> In the creative process there is the father, the author of the play; the mother, the actor pregnant with the part; and the child, the role to be born. [...] The director helps the process along as a sort of matchmaker (Stanislavsky, 1964).

Following his analogy, once authors have done the deed they are dispensable, and directors may be helpful, but are not essential. Ultimately, actors have the sole responsibility of 'giving birth' to the role. In this way Stanislavsky deemed the actor a creative artist, independent from both the writer and director. The creative independence of the actor was something that Stanislavsky obviously felt very passionately about. For example, when the student Grisha asks in *An Actor Prepares*, 'what is left for the actor since everything is prepared by others? Just trifles?' Tortsov is indignant:

> Do you think that to believe in the imaginative fiction of another person, and to bring it to life, is a trifle? [...] We know of cases where a bad play has achieved world fame because of having been re-created by a great actor. [...] We bring to life what is hidden under the words; we put our

own thoughts into the author's lines, and we establish our own relationships to other characters. [...] We filter through ourselves all the materials that we receive from the author and the director; we work over them, supplementing them out of our own imagination. [...] And as a final result we have truly productive activity. [...] And that tremendous work you tell me is just trifles! No, indeed. That is creativeness and art (Stanislavski, 1963).

Sharon Marie Carnicke is correct in claiming that Stanislavsky 'consistently demands respect for the actor as a creative artist, independent of the author who wrote the play, the designer who envisions it, and the director who stages it' (Carnicke, 1998). There is no doubt that Stanislavsky rated highly the independent creativity of the actor. However, he increasingly conceived of it as *dependent on the director*.

It cannot be overstressed that in Stanislavsky's day, directors were relative new-comers to the theatre. Cast as 'matchmaker', the director may seem indispensable, but writers and actors throughout most of theatre's history got along perfectly well without their services. Rudlin and Paul note that the 'ubiquity of the director in theatre and film is today as unquestioned as that of the sea captain: every ship must have one', but 'when Copeau became a director (*metteur en scène*) in 1913, 'the job had only been thought of as desirable, let alone necessary, for three decades or so' (Rudlin & Paul, 1990). In order to secure their position in theatre production, directors needed to carve out their own creative role. Fabrizio Cruciani makes the point that the fledgling 'director-teachers' aimed 'not only to train students for the theatre, or for their own theatres, but also to forge the implements of their own creativity' (Cruciani, 1991). While the actor becomes the main 'implement' of the director's creativity, the actor's own creativity becomes increasingly dependent on the director, and the part-nership of actor and director is forged as the most significant creative relationship in theatre: Stanislavsky and Olga Knipper, Brecht and Helene Weigel, Grotowski and Ryszard Cieślak are testimonies to this. The upshot: the actor-audience relationship is pre-empted.

The director assumed the role of spokesperson for the author and—as first spec-tator—also became spokesperson for the audience. 'Omniscient' and 'omnipresent', directors positioned themselves at both the beginning and end of the theatrical process, and increasingly actors came to rely on them to mediate: to assume primary responsibility for interpreting the text and for speculating on the spectators. Between text and actor, between audience and actor, the director is now the linchpin of the-atre's creative processes, the point around which it now pivots. I definitely do not wish to argue a case for the dispensability of directors (I rather like them, and enjoy being one), but to make the point that Stanislavsky allocated increasing creative responsibilities to the director, ensuring not only his/her role in interpreting the text, creating the *mise en scène*, orchestrating ensemble playing—but also in the creative processes of the actor.

Stanislavsky's director is crucial to the actor. The director takes care of the big picture, taking care of things which might get in the way of actors achieving their main goal of creating characters. In Stanislavsky's own words, the director assumes responsibility for 'the expressiveness of the over-all performance' and its 'external shaping' (Stanislavski, 1968). This allows the actor to focus on the minutiae of characterisation. But Stanislavsky's job description for directors doesn't end here: the director 'must' also 'facilitate the creativeness of the actors' (Stanislavski, 1968). There are numerous ways in which a director can do this: as inspirational coach or muse, a 'talented director may come along and drop just a word, the actor will catch fire and his role will glow with all the colours of his soul's prism' (Stanislavski, 1977). The director also helps the actor keep on track, making sure that the role 'evolves naturally and only from the artistic kernel of the play' (Stanislavski, 1968). And, in one their most important roles, directors assist actors in the realisation of their characters: helping the actor, for example, 'break down the role into smaller units' and 'separate objectives' (Stanislavski, 1968). Under such direction, actors are nominally left free to concentrate on their characterisations. This, however, may prove less of a boon than it seems: as the creativity of acting is now taken up almost exclusively by character-creation, actors become more and more reliant on directors, and arguably relinquish other facets of their creativity. In *An Actor Prepares*, Tortsov challenges the students:

> Just try to stand up in such a space [an empty space] and pour out the role of Hamlet, Othello, Macbeth! How difficult is it to do without the help of a director, or scheme of movements, without properties that you can lean on (Stanislavski, 1963).

The actor's work has become 'difficult' without the director. Not that directors should, in Stanislavsky's opinion, foist themselves upon 'their' actors, showing 'them all the 'business'', but they have become unquestionably integral to their actor's creativity: 'I have arrived at the conviction that the creative work of the director must proceed in unison with that of the actor' (Stanislavski, 1968).

3.2 Rehearsals: Site of the Actor's Creativity?

It is the creative collaboration of director and actor that becomes the most significant relationship in the theatrical enterprise—a collaboration which, however, does not occur on stage in performance, but, crucially, only in *rehearsal*. The rehearsal is, thus, established as the place where the 'real' creative work of the actor takes place and, consequently, performance becomes marginalized. Post-Stanislavsky, the pre-eminence of the rehearsal in theatrical production may seem 'normal': 'the rehearsal process' has become part of theatrical vernacular and practice, but the extensiveness and complexity of rehearsals are, it must be remembered, a relatively new phenomenon, one that Stanislavsky played a huge part in creating. At the Moscow Art Theatre of the late-1920s and early-1930s, the impact of this new phenomenon was evident. Actor Vasili Toporkov observes:

> During very intensive, very active rehearsal work, nobody gives any thought to the final result, that is, to the final performance; here the future audience is somehow ignored. [...] Much more attention is given to things which the audience will never see (Toporkov, 1954/1998).

Stanislavsky's attention was essentially on the actor in the rehearsal or classroom: the theories, methodologies and techniques are primarily all designed for these arenas. At the Opera-Dramatic Studio in Moscow (1935-1938), 'students spent almost two years studying before they were allowed to begin work on a play', let alone perform one for an audience—two years focused on developing the 'means by which to create and communicate the Dramatic 'I'' (Benedetti, 1998). Rehearsals, according to Stanislavsky in *An Actor Prepares*, should be as long as it takes for the character to reach 'full-term', that is, 'as long as that of a human being'. This is when and where the primary creation occurs.

It can be argued that Stanislavsky's psycho-techniques (relaxation of muscles, concentration of attention, faith and sense of truth, imagination, given circumstances, emotion memory and so forth) are aimed at enabling the actor in performance to induce the 'creative inner state' so that he or she can create anew night after night. Indeed, Stanislavsky recognized that in performance, the actor is not in some kind of creative stasis:

> in our art you must live the part every moment that you are playing it, and every time. Each time it is recreated it must be lived afresh and incarnated afresh (Stanislavski, 1964).

But performance is not considered as being a site of creativity in its own right, one possibly requiring different skills to those needed in the rehearsal. Performance is, at most, when and where a prior creation is '*recreated*'.

It is not difficult to understand why rehearsals should become a privileged site. For theorists and teachers of acting alike, it is much easier to put theories and methods to the test in the laboratory-like environment of the rehearsal and classroom, compared to which the performance situation, with its many variables, tends to frustrate analysis and elude control. Nor is it by accident that the rise of the modern director occurred alongside the rise of the rehearsal. After all, the director's primary creative realm is the rehearsal and beyond here, in performance, he or she is present only by proxy. Gnawing their fingernails to the quick, they are forced to scratch out a few meager, impotent notes and sit in excruciating silence and watch. For some this proves an impossible feat, one which Polish director Tadeusz Kantor got around by sometimes appearing as a 'player' in his productions. Thankfully, Kantor is an exception to the norm.

It must not be overlooked that at the time of formulating his theories and methods, Stanislavsky was primarily a director and teacher: although his work finds its impetus in his experiences as an actor, his success and renown are based on his work as director-teacher. In this role, he would naturally favour the domain in which he could most fully exercise his own creativity. But the unfortunate result is that it is in rehearsal where Stanislavsky conceives the actor's 'real', creative work to take place:

> the actor's work begins with the search for the artistic kernel of the play. This he must transplant to his own soul and from that moment shall begin his creative process. [...] If it is to be a genuine, living process and result in the creation of a living, vivid, truly artistic image [...] much more time is necessary than is usually allowed. [...] That is why in our theatre we do not put on a production after some eight or ten rehearsals [...] but only after dozens of rehearsals which sometimes continue over a period of several months (Stanislavski, 1968).

With this emphasis on rehearsal, performance is occluded as a creative site for the actor. In *An Actor Prepares* the first year passes and the students have not yet performed a play for an audience, only exercises and scenes for colleagues and teachers. The assumption is clear: nothing significant can be learned—or taught—in or about performance. In fact, the performance situation is even considered perilous. Cast out of the safe, laboratory environment of the rehearsal, actors are stranded: 'left to act without direction' and what is more, they must cope with an insidious 'obstacle': the audience. Tortsov's advice to the student-actors could not be clearer:

> You must first discover what the obstacles are, and learn to deal with them. [...] The most important one, as you know, is the abnormal circumstance of an actor's creative work—it must be done in public (Stanislavski, 1964).

As actors become preoccupied with character-identification, and retreat into their own inner worlds, the audience becomes a problematic aspect of the creative processes of acting. Even before Stanislavsky was warning actors about the potentially lethal lure of the audience, Lewes had voiced his concern: audiences disturb 'the artistic imagination of the actor by withdrawing it from its direct object', and frustrate the actor's attempts toward 'imaginatively identifying himself with the character' (Cole & Chinoy, 1970). Following Lewes' lead, Tortsov is adamant:

> 'I hope you will take your minds off the audience';

> 'The magnet of the audience is to be resisted';

> 'Forget about the public. Think about yourself. [...] If you are interested, the public will follow you';

> 'There are still many actors [...] who in defiance of any illusion we can create, by means of light, sounds or colour still feel their interest more centred in the auditorium than on the stage';

> '[T]he stage, with all its attendant publicity, tends to lead actors away from natural, human adaptations to situations, and tempts them to conventional, theatrical ways' (Stanislavski, 1964).

In fact, psycho-techniques such as 'concentration of attention' and 'public solitude' are especially designed to mitigate the potentially disruptive influence of audiences, enabling the actor to retreat into him or herself 'like a snail in its shell' (Stanislavski, 1963).

One must, of course, contextualize Stanislavsky's circumspection regarding audiences. In the first instance, there was his own stage fright. He describes how exercises aimed at focusing in on himself helped him overcome performance anxiety and promote his creativity:

> My public exercises centred my attention on the perceptions and states of my body, at the same time drawing my attention away from what was happening on the other side of the footlights, in the auditorium beyond the black and terrible hole of the proscenium arch. In what I was doing I ceased to be afraid of the audience, and at times forgot that I was on the stage. I noticed that it was especially at such times that my creative mood was most pleasant (Cole & Chinoy, 1970).

Beyond this, Stanislavsky was also countering inherited and outdated acting conventions aimed gratuitously at wooing and wowing audiences. But over one hundred years later and removed from this context, one must be very careful about taking Stanislavsky literally. In the 1970s, Peter Handke may have offended his audience by direct insults, but for Australian director, Aubrey Mellor, the insult is now in a tendency to ignore the audience:

> that whole respect—or need—for an audience has sort of disappeared. And if the public doesn't need to be there, what are we doing? I actually get really offended by theatre where I know that if I walked out it would have no effect on anyone on stage. It's like there's the 'old-fashioned' actor who likes performing, and the new actor who actually prefers the rehearsal room (Macaulay, 2003).

As a man of the theatre, and especially as an actor, Stanislavsky must have known that his fourth-wall, public-solitude acting is for the actor, as well as audiences, only an illusion. In *An Actor Prepares,* when the fictional student Paul argues that actors get nothing from audiences—only '[a]pplause and flowers', Tortsov counters:

> What about laughter, tears, applause during the performance, hisses, excitement! Don't you count them? [...] The audience constitute the spiritual acoustics for us. They give back what they receive from us as living, human emotions (Stanislavski, 1964).

Tortsov even goes as far to suggest that an audience can inspire the actor's creativity: a 'crowd of spectators oppresses and terrifies an actor, but it also rouses his truly creative energy'. Advising novice actors, Stanislavsky is unequivocal:

> take your places beside us in front of the footlights more often. The things I am talking about are not learned in the classroom, in rehearsals, or in working at home. They are learned principally in front of the footlights, before a full auditorium, heart to heart, in the very moment of creativeness (Stanislavski, 1968).

What is learned 'in front of the footlights' is, however, never articulated. Unfortunately, Stanislavsky goes no further on the subject, falling short of even gesturing toward a methodology of actor/audience/performance. But it is the heart of the matter: performance is when and where the actor becomes the primary creator. Nicholas Arnold is apposite:

> Notwithstanding the control of preparation and reception by the director, the actor controls production. [...] It is not possible (except perhaps for Tadeusz Kantor) for directors to materialize on stage and polymorphically embody their internal Platonic interpretations. [...] A production is prepared under one set of circumstances. It is performed under another set, which varies night-to-night, moment-to-moment. The messages must, therefore, be continuously re-encoded, so that they are received in the desired way, under differing conditions. It is, of course, at this point that the performance 'realizes' itself, via the actor. Up to now, it has merely been a complex of well-founded conjectures, lacking the audience as the vital articulatory component (Arnold, 1991).

It is in performance that the actor has to embark on a new act of creation—with the audience as complicit and even co-creators. It is ironic, therefore, that while Stanislavsky championed the creativeness of the actor, to a great degree he actually curtailed it, occluding from the actor's repertoire the creative relationship of actor and audience. Masakazu makes the observation that when 'Stanislavski and his successors took the center stage, the audience was always treated as a subordinate factor in performance and was never regarded as an essential part of dramatic creation' (Masakazu, 1984). 'Never' may be too strong a word, but what is certain is that Stanislavsky privileged the creative processes of the rehearsal room. It was there, working with directors that the actor's 'true' creativity resided.

An actor's creativity, however, is not in actuality restricted to collaborating with directors in rehearsal rooms or, even, to character-creation: actors create more than characters and they do so in performances for audiences. Stanislavsky never ventured this far. Nor did his followers. Not the least bequest of Stanislavsky to Western theatre is to have drawn the line on the actor's creativity this side of performance. It is a line which remains firmly in place in actor-training, where Stanislavsky's legacy, combined with professional pedagogies, have served to establish a hegemonic—and restrictive—practice.

4 CREATICS: Performance-Oriented Training

Combing the curricula and syllabi of the contemporary conservatory schools, it would appear at first sight that their training programs are performance-oriented, extending from rehearsal into production. Esteemed training institutions such as the National Institute of Dramatic Art and the Western Australian Academy of Performing Arts in Australia; the Bristol Old Vic Theatre School and the Royal Academy of Dramatic Art in England; and the Juilliard Drama Division in the United States not only provide production-based training but maintain that productions 'are a fundamental component' (Western Australian Academy of Performing Arts, 2001). In this respect, they are true to the Michel Saint-Denis' prototype from which they all heavily draw. Saint-Denis considered that training for training's sake was potentially detrimental: student-actors should, in his view, always be focussed on the production of plays as their final goal. Starting with studio or black-box productions with minimal or no production elements, the training in his model school would culminate in the final year with full-scale productions. By the end of their three years, students would have acted in nine productions 'crowned by a two-week repertory season' (Saint-Denis, 1982). Following Saint-Denis' lead, the aforementioned schools all have busy production schedules, because pedagogically it is in productions that students 'put all that has been learned so far in the classwork into practice before audiences' (Bristol Old Vic Theatre School, n.d.). Head of Acting at Australia's National Institute of Dramatic Art (NIDA), Tony Knight, comments:

> The performances are the climax of the term's work; we are not into too many sheltered workshops. [...] The practical application of skills and methods is the central focus (personal communication, August 30, 2007).

However, closer investigation of the schools' courses, the curricula and the Saint-Denis prototype upon which they are based reveals a picture in which the emphasis remains, in fact, primarily focused on *rehearsal* processes and not on *performance*, and where a *production-oriented* training does not, in fact, equate to a *performance-oriented* one. The crucial difference between them may not be immediately apparent: a production-oriented training, ostensibly, aims at performance, but conceives of it as a place where the actors *show*, *present* or *transfer* what they have achieved in the rehearsal or classroom onto the stage. In other words, performances become *presentations* or *showings* of a prior creation. According to Ellis Jones (former Head of Acting at the Royal Academy of Dramatic Art), students in contemporary acting schools can anticipate a training which includes among other things '[r]ehearsing for presentations' (Jones, 1998). Saint-Denis is unequivocal: 'students will learn to act by rehearsing plays' (Saint-Denis, 1982). What is learnt rehearsing plays and in class is then simply *transplanted* or *transferred* to the performance situation. The successful student, according to the acting curriculum at the Western Australian Academy of

Performing Arts, demonstrates 'the ability to transfer rehearsed material into performance' (Western Australian Academy of Performing Arts, 2001). The implication is clear: performing requires no additional skills. In this *production*–oriented training, performance is conceived as an event towards which the training is directed, but for which student actors are not specifically trained. What is assumed is that competence in rehearsals will translate into successful performances. If one accepts this assumption, performances serve as rubber-stamps for a prior creation, but are not acts of creation in themselves. The corollary to this: audiences exist only to validate the rehearsal process.

What I call a *performance*-oriented course, on the other hand, would conceive of performance not as validation of rehearsal work, but as what it is: a creative site, if not the most important creative site in theatre. This raises some obvious questions: *what is required for training for performance?* More fundamentally, *is it possible to teach it?* The answer to this last question would appear to be 'yes, it is'. Traditional Asian training praxes, for example, all train actors for performance. James Brandon comments that 'most Asian actor training' is 'first skill centered and then audience centered' (Brandon, 1989). It is not concerned with creativity in rehearsals or the creative relationship between actors and directors—both rehearsals and director being as good as non-existent. The focus of the training is entirely on acquiring the appropriate skills for creating performances for audiences. Can we take a lesson from this? I think we owe it to student actors in the West to at least investigate the possibility of training for performance. Such an investigation would have the potential to enrich the creative scope of their acting, aiming at not only making them good *actors*, but also good *performers*.

This is the aim and scope of *CREATICS'* exercises and strategies: to develop actors' creativity in performance. The methodology takes actors through four main competencies:
- *situation awareness*
- *audience awareness*
- *divided consciousness*
- *presence*

4.1 Situation Awareness

'*creative people tend to have less focused attention than uncreative people*' (Martindale, 1995).

My Stanislavsky training taught me to focus intently on fulfilling my objectives. My peers and I were all familiar with the 'Hindu Tale' in *An Actor Prepares,* where a Maharajah chooses a minister based on his capacity to concentrate whilst walking 'around on top of the city walls, holding a dish full to the brim with milk without spilling a drop'. The successful candidate managed to do this even though his concentration was tested by all sorts of distractions, including gunshots. 'Did you hear the shots?' asked the Maharajah. 'No, I was watching the milk', was the reply. Likewise I sought such focus and concentration. Over time, however, I discovered that this type of intense focus was not useful for me in performance. What actors need, especially in performance, is *full-situation awareness*.

In the *Cambridge Handbook of Expertise and Expert Performance*, Mica Endsley maintains that *situation awareness* is 'a critical cornerstone for expertise in most domains'. She defines situation awareness as 'the perception of the elements in the environment within a volume of time and space, the comprehension of their meaning and the projection of their status in the near future' (Endsley, 2006). I often urge my students to watch sport and observe how good sportsmen and women manage to maintain focus on their own role *and* at the same time 'read the play', that is, have awareness of what is happening on the whole field. In fact, how they play from moment to moment is informed by this awareness of the whole situation. Likewise, I encourage students to remain committed to their character or task objectives *and* open to what is happening around them. It is not a question of being committed *or* being open to other options. Rather, as Bogart and Landau claim, both commitment *and* openness are possible—and are, in fact, essential: '[b]eing fully committed yet open to change simultaneously' liberates the actor, allowing them to become more creative (Bogart & Landau, 2005). Phillip Zarrilli uses the term 'the body becomes all eyes' to encapsulate 'that ideal state of embodiment and accomplishment' of actors. In *Psychophysical Acting*, he writes that when 'one's body is all eyes then like Lord Brahman the thousand eyed, one is like an animal—able to see, hear, and respond immediately to any stimulus in the immediate environment' (Zarrilli, 2009).

Possessing a highly receptive, wide-ranging attention enables actors to multiply their choices, and maximizing choices is a characteristic of all creative acts. Dean Keith Simonton observes that:

> Most significantly and consistently, creativity is positively associated with openness to experience. [...] This inclination is also related to the creative person's capacity for defocused attention. This is the capacity that enables the mind to encompass simultaneously two or more unrelated stimuli or associations, thus enabling the mind to conceive ideational combinations impossible under more focused attention (Simonton, 2004).

When it comes to acting, Saint-Denis makes the point forcefully:

> Acting requires the right sort of concentration. Once the student has discovered the results that can be obtained through concentration, he tends, in improvisation, to over-concentrate and through that to become passive and constrained, in a word, constipated. He may obtain a *kind* of truth but it has no performance value (Saint-Denis, 1982).

> ### The Body is All Eyes
>
> The following *CREATICS'* exercise can be used working on scenes in rehearsals or in training workshops.
>
> 1. Actors play a scene with their attention on maintaining eye contact: '*Lock eyes with your acting partner. Don't let anything else distract you from keeping eye contact. Feel the connection, feel the energy that passes between you and your partner.*'
> 2. They play the scene again, shifting their attention to different parts of the body: '*Shift your eyes to your feet*'. '*Play the scene as if your eyes are in your belly*'. '*Act and react with the back of your neck.*' All the time eye contact is maintained.
> 3. They then allow their field of vision to expand: '*Let your focus soften. You don't have to keep your eyes locked on your partner's eyes. Let other things in your environment come into your field of vision. Don't seek them out—let them come and allow yourself to respond to them*'. However, '*While your awareness is now expanding to take in your playing environment, try and keep the connection you achieved, the energy that passed between you and your partner when your eyes were locked. Maintain the sense that your every move and breath is being observed by your partner.*
> 4. Finally, the scene is played again, with the actors whispering. When they are listening with every inch of their bodies, they move into full voice.
>
> I came across the usefulness of whispering scenes by accident. I was rehearsing in a studio next to a theatre where a show was in progress. Time was precious, so rather than cancel the rehearsal, we proceeded and the actors whispered their lines. What I observed was that they were forced to listen—really listen to each other, using every part of the body to sense their partners and to pick up not only what was being said but also any physical cues or signals. The corollary to this was that the actors whispering had to articulate clearly and engage their whole body in order to successfully communicate. In this heightened state of full-body awareness, they became super-sensitive not only to their partners but the space around them.

'It has no performance value'—that is the crux of the matter. Because as any actor knows, they might be able to focus their attention solely on their objectives, their actions, their 'make-believe' world in rehearsal, but in *performance* this is just not possible. Performance just won't allow it. In performance, actors require a more broadly ranging and expansive attention. Shelley Russell-Parks gives a wonderful example of what is needed: playing Blanche in *A Streetcar Named Desire,* at the height of emotional intensity, she had to undergo a complete costume change offstage, while simultaneously continuing the dialogue with Stella onstage:

> I had to learn to open the door precisely enough to expose my face, but not so much as to expose the woman doing my hair. Furthermore, I had to raise one arm to allow a second assistant to zip a side zipper (Russell-Parks, 1989).

Rather than being a distraction, Russell-Parks says the offstage 'invasion' of her costume and hair 'became part of the playworld's immediate focus'. She concludes: the actor in performance needs to be aware of much more than the character and the 'play-world's environment', but also the 'theatre, audience, and acting all become apparent to the perceiving consciousness'.

To achieve expertise in performance, *full* situation awareness is required; actors need to 'listen' to their total performance space, which includes *an auditorium of spectators*.

4.2 Audience Awareness

actor and audience are 'the indispensable elements in making theatre for three concentrated hours. Everyone else [...] is a voyeur' (Mackintosh, 1993).

As a young actor, I conceived of audiences as the *other* and our relationship as *us* versus *them*. I never thought they were part of what I was doing out there. In fact, my Stanislavsky-based training encouraged me to treat audiences as an obstacle. In psychologically realistic acting, the actor's job is to create a character presumably behaving as in real life. Creative actors are, therefore, deemed to be those who seemingly block out the audience and who, according to Bella Merlin, 'preserve nature's creative freedom' by connecting 'with a more useful onstage objective' (Merlin, 2005). Actors are commonly advised that their 'world is the acting space' and where their 'concentration should be, not backstage, not in the audience but there in the make-believe world we have created' (Benedetti, 1998). In Stanislavsky's own words:

> as soon as the actor stops paying any attention to him, the spectator will begin to show an interest in him, especially if the actor himself is interested in something on the stage that the audience, too, finds important (Stanislavsky, 1973).

In my training we did perform in front of audiences, but in the first and second years it was limited to faculty members and fellow students. In front of this 'in-house' audience, it is believed that students are free to experiment and put their newly learned skills to the test without the risks of potentially damaging public censure. Ellis Jones puts the case:

> For the first two years, schools discourage exposure. [...] When you are going through a period of intense training your focus is on your equipment and you need the space to make mistakes out of the spotlight (Jones, 1998).

Saint-Denis was of the same opinion, preferring not even to use the word 'performance' so as to avoid putting any untoward pressure on the students:

In the beginning of the training we call any performance the students give a showing, and not a performance. The reason is that we want to encourage the student's concentration, and leave him free to make, with guidance, the connection between his inner existence and his means of expression, without disturbing him with the feeling that he has to prove himself. The important thing in the first year is to plant the roots of the actor's invention at the deepest possible level (Saint-Denis, 1982).

While this is understandable, especially in the early part of the training, it has worrying implications: namely, that performance is not seen as a potential spark to 'the actor's invention', or even an integral part of the actor's process. Just as alarming and in addition to this, audiences are restricted to the role of critics and judges, who exist only to validate students' work. They are not vital participants in a theatrical event, let alone conceived as possible co-conspirators or co-creators.

It might seem that these caveats apply only to the early days of the training and '[e]ventually, the day comes when the student actors have the chance they've been waiting for: to get out there in front of an audience and do it!' (Brown, 1996). Generally, this day comes toward the end of the student's penultimate year with black-box productions for 'invited guests', and then in the final year with full-scale productions open to the 'general public'. It is in the final phase of the training that students are believed ready to come out of the 'hot-house' and perform for a general public audience. The 'emphasis shifts' at the end of the third year, according to the Juilliard course description, 'from the laboratory to the theatre, with the addition of costume, makeup, lighting, music, and some scenery'—and an audience (Juilliard, n.d.). The audience is an 'added extra', like the other production elements and, once again, the notion that audiences are not integral to the acting process is reinforced.

This is the significant omission in current mainstream training: there is no serious 'speculation on the spectators', on the role *audiences* play in the actor's creative processes. Therefore, it is hardly surprising that for many student-actors an *us* versus *them* attitude develops and becomes entrenched. Actor David Warrilow makes this point:

There was a time when my perception of the audience was 'us' and 'them'. [...] I therefore was for a long time in the position of investing a great deal of energy in defending what I was doing against supposed criticism (Lassiter, 2002).

Warrilow goes on to say he 'was so full of anxiety and insecurity' that he 'was not able to enter into the proper flow of the exchange' which he now believes 'it can and ideally must be' (Lassiter, 2002).

Stand-Up!

Stand-Up is a terrific—and terrifying—way of coming to realise the two-way street between actors and audience. There are many ways of approaching Stand-Up and developing a routine. I find using neutral masks a good way to start. Stand-Up often focuses on the performer's idiosyncrasies and the Stand-Up persona is often a heightened version of oneself, so this exercise is a great way to draw actors' attention to their own mannerisms.

1. Wearing a neutral mask, actors individually walk from upstage to downstage, whilst the other actors observe very carefully their walk and other physical traits that stand out. In a mask, the actors find that their own particular walk and physical idiosyncrasies are highlighted.
2. The observers then mirror the walk of the walker, who then observes his or her walk re-enacted by the others, and taking it on board, copies this re-enacted walk, moving from upstage to downstage again.
3. The observers mirror the walk a second time, but this time they exaggerate it—and the walker takes on this exaggerated walk, moving from upstage to downstage again.
4. This process is repeated one more time with the degree of exaggeration increased to the max.
5. When all actors have walked their walk and had it mirrored back to them three times, with increasing exaggeration, they take off the masks and walk their walk all together in the space. Using the numbers one to ten (ten being over-the-top exaggeration), they increase or decrease the exaggeration.
6. The actors then think of something that they either love or hate, and think of three reasons why they love or hate this thing. At this stage, this does not have to be funny.
7. They then put together the physicality they found earlier with their loves or hates and reasons, and rehearse this germ of a Stand-Up routine.
8. They now perform these mini routines to each other and then at the end discuss what they found out about themselves: *'What is peculiar and special about you?'*
9. This exercise can be extended, with the actors being given a number of weeks to develop and rehearse their routines for a public performance. Whilst this is nerve-wracking for most—*'the scariest thing I have ever done'*—what they learn about the 'flow of the exchange' between the performer and audience, the confidence they gain in this exchange, is invaluable.

Many actors and directors believe that the relationship between actor and audience, the 'flow of the exchange', is the essence of theatre, its base denominator. John Gielgud said this: 'nothing really matters except the actual momentary contact between actor and audience' (Cole & Chinoy, 1970). In 'The Theatre's New Testament', Grotowski goes further and actually defines theatre as essentially 'what takes place between spectator and actor' (Grotowski & Barba, 2002). Theatre 'cannot exist without the actor-spectator relationship of perceptual, direct, 'live' communion' (Grotowski, 2002). Director Anne Bogart concurs:

The theatre is what happens between spectator and actor. The actor is completely dependent upon the creative potential of each audience member and must be able to adjust and respond to whatever ensues. The actor initiates and the audience completes the circle with their imagination, memory and creative sensibilities (Bogart, 2001).

Walking the Auditorium

Walking is an integral part of many actor-training methods. This simple *CREATICS'* strategy takes walking that one step further: into the auditorium. It's great for opening nights, and I find it particularly useful when you are in a theatre you are not familiar with. On tour, you can play a different theatre almost every night and this walking exercise helps make the big black hole out there familiar:

1. Firstly, walk the stage and then the auditorium. While walking the auditorium, maintain an awareness of the stage and when on the stage sense the auditorium.
2. Then, only walk the auditorium. Open up to this space: feel it envelop you. Sit in different seats and soak up the atmosphere. '*What does the stage look like from Row 12 Seat 3? Who might be sitting in this seat tonight? What will they expect? What will they see?*' Explore the auditorium's nooks and crannies and do all this while always maintaining an awareness of the stage area.
3. Return to walking the stage area only—and keep your awareness of the auditorium.

Given the obvious vitality of the actor-audience relationship, why then has it been marginalized in actor training?

A fundamental reason lies within the hegemonic theatre praxis of psychological realism and its demand that actors should behave *naturally*, as if in *real* life. The audience has no place here except as voyeurs. Sitting in a darkened auditorium, it is easy for audiences to become invisible and, conversely, the lit actors to retreat more easily into their fictional world. There were and are those who 'have sought (rather than allowed) a central role for the spectator' (Bennett, 1997). Yet, despite these enterprises, in mainstream theatre with its predominant fare of psychologically realistic plays:

> performers are set apart and audiences asked to respond cognitively and emotionally in predefined categories of approval, disapproval, arousal or passivity. Audience interaction with the performers may enhance it, but it is not meant nor allowed to become part of its definition (Dayan & Katz, 1994).

However, as all actors know, even in psychological realism there is a direct (albeit subtle) dialogue between their audiences and them. Nicholas Arnold puts it eloquently:

> Any performer knows that the conventional active/passive relationship between actor and audience is, in fact, a constantly shifting relationship between equals, signalled and sustained

by a continuous interchange of messages between the two parties, which re-adjusts the relationship as the performance is developed in time and space (Arnold, 1991).

Gathering the Eyes

Gathering the eyes of the audience is an image I have found extremely useful in helping actors engage with their audiences. The phrase comes from a story told to me by theatre director, playwright and academic David George about Noh Actor Akira Matsui (personal communication, April 19, 2005). In an interview with George, Matsui spoke about 'gathering the eyes of the audience', literally scanning the audience behind his mask and making eye contact one by one. I use this figuratively, as an image actors can use to draw in the audience to what they are doing on stage—an invitation to the audience to be present with them.

The actors do this exercise one-by-one for the rest of the group:

1. While the actor stands off-stage, he or she is asked the following questions: '*At this moment, where is your energy coming from? Where is its source, in what part of your body? Feel your energy like a flame, flickering. Let this flame grow and when it has reached the point when you want to propel yourself onto the stage—stop. Gather your energy, gather yourself—but don't let the flame reduce. Keep it burning strong.*'

2. The actor then walks onto the stage, feeling all eyes on him/her with every step: '*If you feel you have lost the gaze of the audience, stop and gather it in.*'

3. On reaching centre-stage, the actor stands still, and when he or she feels that: '*you have gathered the eyes and drawn the audience into your space, introduce yourself. Say your name. When you feel your name has settled in the audience's mind, turn and exit, all the time sensing the audiences' eyes on your back.*'

Audience is vital to the creative process. All creative acts, according to Csikszentmihalyi, are 'constructed through an *interaction between producer and audience*' (Csikszentmihalyi, 1999). He maintains that the 'audience is as important to [creativity's] constitution as the individual to whom it is credited'. This is consistent with what theorists in other disciplines have argued. For example, while Mikel Dufrenne acknowledges the independent existence of the 'work of art', what he defines as 'the aesthetic object exists only [...] as it is experienced by the spectator' (Dufrenne, 1973). Roland Barthes asserts that reception is where meanings are ultimately created: 'a text's unity lies not in its origins but in its destination' (Barthes, 1984).

The stage actor's creativity is derived, in no small measure, from the interaction with his or her audience. This in turn means that actors should 'speculate' on the spectator, and not totally relinquish this creative responsibility to directors. Directors, faced by multiple choices of blocking, rhythm, colour, and so forth have almost always made their decisions in terms of a wished-for audience response. Michael Chekhov quotes Yevgeny Vakhtangov:

From the first rehearsal, I imagine the theatre filled with the audience. When giving my suggestions or demonstrating to the actor this or that passage, I 'hear' and 'see' clearly the reaction of the imaginary audience and reckon with it. Very often I quarrel with the imaginary audience and insist upon my point of view' (Chekhov, 1991).

Anne Bogart is unequivocal about the central role the audience plays in her own creativity. In *A Director Prepares,* she writes that 'the fundamental issue that lies at the heart of the creative act' is 'the artist's intention *vis-à-vis* the audience'. If the actor is, therefore, to be deemed an artist, they too should not be exempt from asking the question: *'what is my intention vis-à-vis the audience?'*

Arguably, the answer to this question is already important in rehearsal, but it is imperative in performance, where the actor assumes primary responsibility for communicating with an audience and maintaining that communication. Director Aubrey Mellor reminds actors that they 'have to move into the act of communicating. Doing it! And night after night!' (Macaulay, 2003). In part, what the actor communicates is circumscribed by the text and direction, but there is much more that is needed to engage an audience. Nicholas Arnold makes the point:

> It is also up to the actor to use manipulative devices to achieve the focus demanded by the director, and implied in the text of the writer. An actor may be dressed in red, while all the others are in black, be at the top of a flight of stairs in a spotlight, the recipient of the gaze and gesture of the entire company: but if the actor does not, firstly, engage techniques to acknowledge this focus, and then further techniques to maintain it, the focus loses significance, and will disappear (Arnold, 1991).

Letting the Audience in on Your Act

1. The actors choose a simple everyday activity (e.g. texting, putting on shoes, writing a note, entering the room...). If they are rehearsing, they can choose an activity they need to perform as part of their roles. They can use props if they need to, but are instructed not to mime.
2. They rehearse this activity with the intention of making it as precise and 'legible' as possible: *'Are you blurring some moments? Rushing through? Be clear and precise in your movements. Isolate the individual movements that make up your activity. Don't rush through them. Make them full and exact. Give them their due weight.'*
3. The actors then add Given Circumstances and observe how this changes their activities.
4. They then add stakes: *'If you don't complete this activity, what is at stake? Not much? A lot? How does this change how you perform the activity?'*
5. The actors perform their tasks with utmost and undivided attention: *'All your senses, your whole body and mind are focussed 100% on performing your task.'*
6. They then perform their tasks using peripheral vision: *'Allow yourself to extend your attention to the space immediately around. At all times remain focused on performing your task.'*
7. The actors are then instructed to *'extend your attention to the full playing space. Don't focus on anyone or anything in particular. Keep your attention on performing your task.'*

8. Then they: *'alternate between placing your attention in as tight an area as possible. As if you are in a spotlight. Now expand your attention to the whole space, the whole room, with all the other bodies in it, doing their own things. Don't focus on anyone or anything in particular. Keep your attention on performing your task.'*

9. They then observe themselves performing their activities as if *'you are a member of the audience. What is your spectator seeing?'*

10. The actors each whisper a running commentary in the third person from an audience perspective as they perform their tasks. For example, *'She is slowly moving towards the letter. She looks back to the door. She pauses for a moment, looking at the door. Who is she expecting? She looks worried. She suddenly rushes to the letter...'*

11. Finally, the actors perform their activity for the rest of the class. The audience is instructed to ask: *'What is the actor doing to make this activity watchable? When do you lose interest?'*

Desired performance outcomes are negotiated and established in collaboration with the director and fellow-actors in rehearsals. After all, among its multiple meanings, performance is 'the general success of the activity in light of some standard of achievement' (Carlson, 1996). However, Carlson points out that, beyond this, and possibly 'even more significantly, the task of judging the success of the performance [...] is in these cases not the responsibility of the performer but the observer'. What this implies for actors is that in order to be successful performers, they must gauge their performances not only in light of desired outcomes but also in relation to actual audience responses. They must be able to read or listen to their audiences in order to monitor, calibrate and create successful performances. In order to achieve this they must be their own directors. Instructing his students on how to 'master the conventions of the stage', Stanislavsky's Tortsov reminds them: '[r]emember that I have told you more than once that every actor must be his own director' (Stanislavski, 1961). It is crucial for actors to engage in this sort of speculation—and going even further, attempt to see themselves as the spectator might.

Sitting on Your Shoulder

Michael Chekhov maintained that by peeking 'at himself in his private life, observing how he walks, how he speaks, what gestures he uses in his everyday life', the actor can develop divided consciousness and 'gradually experience the other part of his being as an artistic ego, as his Creative Individuality, as the possessor of the instrument' (Chekhov, 1991).

Actors should set aside time during their day when engaged in everyday activities such as driving, hanging out the washing, cooking, speaking with a friend—and watch themselves from the 'outside'. It is as if their 'outer eye' is like a film camera, circling around them, allowing them to see themselves from all angles— from behind, above, below, front, sides: *'While you watch yourself, retain awareness of what you are doing at all times!'*

This is a very simple exercise, which in time often becomes a natural way of being for an actor— and is an essential way of being in performance.

It is obviously difficult (some would say impossible) for the actor to observe his or her work. Richard Hornby makes the point that the 'problem traditionally with learning how to act has always been that an actor unlike a painter, composer, or novelist cannot experience his or her own work from the audience's viewpoint' (Hornby, 2007). Given this obstacle, it is somewhat surprising, according to Hornby, that video cameras have not been utilized to a far greater extent in acting classes. In the past, it seems that actors used available resources: Diderot's ideal actor, for example, had 'learnt before a mirror every particle of his despair' (Diderot, 1830/1957), and Archer cites Wilson Barrett to stress the importance of actors having a good grasp of their 'outward expression' (Archer, 1888/1957). Barrett comments:

> I have again and again held a mirror to a young actor, and when he has evidently been feeling deeply, his face, to his astonishment, has borne a peaceful, placid smile (Archer, 1888/1957).

Post-Stanislavsky, however, the idea of the actor observing him or herself from the outside, as a spectator might, is commonly perceived as being counter-productive and inhibiting of the actor's creativity. In *An Actor Prepares*, Tortsov considered the practice of using mirrors positively 'dangerous', stressing to his students: *'[y]ou must be very careful in the use of a mirror. It teaches an actor to watch the outside rather than the inside of his soul'*.

In mainstream actor training in the West, students are not generally encouraged to speculate on their external effects. Declan Donnellan, for example, advises the actor against asking questions such as: '[d]oes it look awful when I put my hand on the balcony like this?' He assumes that the answer is 'pure speculation, because none of us can ever know what we look like [...] can never be sure of the effect we are having' (Donnellan, 2002). However, for actors to be able to gauge their effects, especially in performance, the ability to see themselves as an audience might would appear to be highly advantageous. It is most definitely encouraged in many Eastern performance traditions. In the fifteenth century, Noh actor and theorist, Zeami wrote that the actor must 'have come to an ability to see himself as the spectators do' (Zeami, 1984). This advice, argues James Brandon 'could well apply to any genre of Asian theatre: the actor must always be aware of and respond to the mood of the spectator, he must see himself as the audience sees him [...] and adjust his performance accordingly'

(Brandon, 1989). It might be impossible for the actor to have a completely objective picture of him or herself, but difficult though it might be, Zeami maintained that the actor must strive to develop this ability for aesthetic detachment. Through 'assiduous training', according to Zeami, the actor must learn to 'grasp his own internalized outer image' (Zeami, 1984). According to Kunio Komparu, 'only when this happens is he truly able to perceive himself as a performer' (Komparu, 1983).

The importance placed on the actor's ability to see him or herself from the outside is not restricted to non-Western traditions. Michael Chekhov, for instance, comments that the actor must 'develop the habit of seeing himself objectively as an outsider' (Chekhov, 1991). Indeed, if anything distinguishes actors in performance and is a major foundation of their creative work, then it is this one very special ability. After all, as Carlson notes, by definition, performance is 'all activity carried out with a consciousness of itself' (Carlson, 1996). This being the case, the actor in performance must develop an ability for what is variously described as 'detached vision', 'aesthetic perception', 'multiple awareness', or 'divided consciousness'.

4.3 Divided Consciousness

The actor 'must have in himself an unmoved and disinterested onlooker' (Diderot, 1830/1957).

Diderot was the first Western theatre theorist to describe divided consciousness in detail. Since Diderot, discussions of the actor's divided or dual consciousness have frequently resurfaced. Charles Marowitz makes the point that the concept of 'the actor's dual consciousness' was 'exhaustively discussed by Brecht in his writings on the Epic Theatre', informed 'Grotowski's notion of the I-I (the actor who acts and the same actor who 'looks on')', and 'refloated by Michael Chekhov in the late-thirties as divided consciousness' (Marowitz, 1997). When it came to the importance of the actor's divided consciousness, Chekhov was adamant. In a lecture in 1941, he made the point that 'when we are possessed by the part and almost kill our partners and break chairs, etc., then we are not free and it is not art but hysterics'. He went on to say:

> At one time in Russia we thought that if we were acting we must forget everything else. Of course, it was wrong. Then some of our actors came to the point where they discovered that real acting was when we could act and be filled with feelings, and yet be able to make jokes with our partners—two consciousnesses (Chamberlain, 2010).

For Chekhov, 'divided consciousness' is crucial to acting, representing none other than the fourth and final stage of the actor's creative process. It is the 'happy moment' of inspiration when the actor 'becomes inwardly free of his own creation and becomes observer of his own work'. This, according to Chekhov, is 'the aim of the whole creative process, the true desire of the higher Ego of the actor. The conscious now stands divided' (Chekhov, 1991). Chekhov cites Rudolf Steiner:

> 'The actor must not be possessed by his role,' wrote Rudolf Steiner. 'He must stand facing it so that his part becomes objective. He experiences his own creation. With his ego, he stands beside his creation, and is still able to enjoy its extreme joys and sorrows, as if he were facing the outer world' (Chekhov, 1991).

Divided consciousness, in Michael Chekhov's view, is not only central to the actor's creativity, but is instrumental in defining the actor as a creative artist: cultivating the 'habit of seeing himself objectively as an outsider', the actor 'will gradually experience the other part of his being as an artistic ego, as his Creative Individuality' (Chekhov, 1991). It is this capacity, this aesthetic distance or artistic consciousness, which characterizes all artists and all creative acts. Chekhov makes the point, once again quoting Steiner:

> 'Goethe was always in such a division of his personality. He was Goethe whose love was not weaker than that of anyone else, but at the same time he was Goethe who observed. Goethe could always draw back, out and from himself, feeling and contemplating his own experience' (Chekhov, 1991).

Michel Saint-Denis also rated divided consciousness as a crucial capacity of the actor. His major concern with Stanislavsky's psycho-technique was that it 'encouraged too interior an approach whereby the actor may become prisoner of his or her concentration, thus losing crucial, critical detachment' (Baldwin, 2003). For Saint-Denis, the 'actor must develop a kind of double concentration: he must be completely *in* what he is doing, but, at the same time, he must control his way of doing it' (Saint-Denis, 1982). This 'double concentration', according to Saint-Denis, is 'one of the essential secrets of acting'. In order to develop divided consciousness in his students, he advocated mask work. Mask work is routinely used to develop full-body expressivity in the actor, to rid gestures and movements of any unnecessary fussiness or idiosyncrasies, and to overcome debilitating self-consciousness. Saint-Denis, however, also used mask work to develop 'double concentration'. In *Training for the Theatre*, he writes: 'mask work is central to the training precisely because it enables the student to warm his feelings and cool his head'. This allows the actor:

> to experience, in its most startling form, the chemistry of acting. At the very moment when the actor's feelings beneath the mask are at their height, the urgent necessity to control his physical actions compels him to detachment and lucidity (Saint-Denis, 1982).

Masks

This exercise is designed for working on scenes where general blocking had been established and the actors are familiar with their lines.

The actors play the scene in order to reacquaint themselves with it.

1. They then play it masked and silently. Ask them to: *'Put your attention on your every movement and gesture.'* This usually means that they slow right down and their movements and gestures get more pronounced and often bigger. *'If you want to go back over a movement, repeat it—do it.'* The actors are encouraged to engage with how they are moving through the space, how they are still in the space and with their acting partners.
2. Finally, without masks, they play the scene with the words while retaining their attention on their physical actions and those of their scene partners.

Diderot was one of the first to advocate the cultivation of divided consciousness: his ideal actor was one that 'is capable of detached observation like all geniuses' (Roach, 1985). He observed that *repetition* is useful in facilitating this divided consciousness. In a time when extensive rehearsals were not yet common, Diderot saw the potential of repeating. He maintained that through rehearsing or repeating (the French for 'rehearsal' being *répétition*) the blocking, movements, gestures, lines and so forth, the entire role becomes habituated or automatic, enabling the actor to detach and attend to other things that may arise in the performance situation. Ironically, the drilling of a role so that it becomes second nature allows the actor, according to Diderot, to become more open and spontaneous in performance. From a contemporary point of view, Mica Endsley has found that recent research into performance in all fields shows:

> The decrease in demand on mental resources associated with automaticity of physical tasks provides a boon for situation awareness, leaving more attention and working memory for attending to information and forming situation awareness (Endsley, 2006).

However, speaking to other acting teachers and from my own experience, I have found that when teaching you are often under pressure not to repeat exercises or activities. There are always some student-actors who consider repeating exercises a backwards step, or at the very least, boring. But there is no escaping the fact that acting involves repetition, and the actor must learn to love repetition. Indeed, all creative acts involve varying degrees of repetition. Howard Gruber maintains that 'if one looks closely at almost any creative process, one sees a great deal of repetitive work' (Gruber, 1989). Linda Jeffrey writes:

> Repetitive activity is as essential in creative work as it is in everyday life. [...] Sometimes [it] reflects simply the practical need to do the same thing yet again. [...] Sometimes it is undertaken

deliberately as part of an exploration of a complex enterprise. Each time we re-view something we re-vise it, seeing new aspects of the same thing (Jeffrey, 1989).

Jeffrey makes the important observation that, in fact, 'exact repetition is almost impossible. [...] When we try to do exactly the same thing, we do it from the standpoint of the present, which includes every nuance of *this* moment, even including the fact that we have just done 'it' before. So 'it' evolves'. This is a crucial point: no act can ever be the same and each time we repeat, there is the potential to discover something new.

Repetition, in other words, is a useful tool for cultivating the ability to stand outside oneself, and watch: *'What happens when I have an argument with my lover— how do I breathe, what do I look like, do my nostrils flare, do I storm about, or am I still, do I shout or am I quiet?'* However, while this artistic detachment may be part of the preparation phase for many actors, it is crucial to all actors in performance. In order to monitor their work in performances—from ensuring the basics of being heard and seen—actors must, and do, 'sit on their own shoulders'. This is a considerable feat: actors, and performing artists in general, unlike other artists, do not have the luxury of time to stand back and contemplate their work: they must do it instantly, simultaneously creating and assessing their creation at the very moment of reception. How this physically or mentally occurs is open to speculation and many scientific and psychological theories have been postulated. Toward the end of the 1800s, George Henry Lewes, for example, described divided consciousness as 'a rapid alternation of attention from one level of consciousness to another, not unlike the alternating current in standard electrical devices' (Roach, 1985). On the other hand, his contemporary Henry Irving conceived of 'double consciousness' occurring simultaneously:

It is necessary to this art that the mind should have, as it were, a double consciousness, in which all the emotions proper to the occasion may have full swing, while the actor is all the time on the alert for every detail of his method (Taylor, 1989).

To date, the question of whether attention is alternating—and therefore sequential, as Lewes suggested—or whether, as Irving argued, one has the capacity to hold multiple attentions simultaneously remains unanswered. In *The Psychology of Attention*, Harold Pashler concludes that whether divided consciousness or attention occurs in parallel strands or sequentially remains inconclusive, but this notwithstanding, there is evidence to support its existence (Pashler, 1998). Within neuroscience, the 'split-brain' research conducted by Roger Sperry and his associates has opened up the possibility of a 'scientific basis for the dual self' (Lee, 1993). The jury might be out on how it works, but what appears conclusive is that divided attention or consciousness is phenomenologically beyond question (Lee, 1993). Ernest Hilgard asserts that the '[u]nity of consciousness is illusory', rather we all do 'more than one thing at a time—all the time' (Hilgard, 1986). If this is the case of everybody in their everyday lives, it is doubly the case for performers. In the words of Lee Strasberg, doing 'more

than one thing at a time [...] is always required when an actor is performing on stage'
(Strasberg, 1989).

Evidence that the actor in performance does more, and must do 'more than one
thing' simultaneously, is overwhelming. In *Masks or Faces,* William Archer devotes
an entire chapter, quaintly titled 'Brownies of the Mind', in which he poses the question: 'Can you give any examples of the two or more strata of consciousness, or lines
of thought, which must co-exist in your mind while acting?' He concludes that there
'are many brownies', a 'brownie' being 'a benevolent spirit or goblin' which performs
'useful household work while the family is asleep' (*OED* 'Brownie' *n.* Def. 1):

> one of them may be agonising with Othello, while another is criticising his every tone and gesture,
> a third restraining him from strangling Iago in good earnest, a fourth wondering whether the
> play will be over in time to let him catch his last train (Archer, 1888/1957).

Throughout the chapter, Archer cites examples of actors' divided consciousness.
Janet Achurch, for example, comments that 'the only double line of thought I like to
have on stage is a mental criticism on my own performance: 'I got that exclamation
better than last night' or 'I'm sure I'm playing this scene slower than usual'. Clara
Morris, comments: 'I am keenly alive to Clara Morris, to all the details of the play, to
the other actors and how they act, and to the audience; another about the play and
the character I represent'. One of the most famous actresses of the day, Fanny Kemble,
observes that the 'curious part of acting, to me, is the sort of double process which
the mind carries on at once, the combined operation of one's faculties, so to speak, in
diametrically opposite directions'. She goes on to state that:

> [i]t is this watchful faculty (perfectly prosaic and commonplace in its nature), which never
> deserts me while I am uttering all that exquisite passionate poetry in Juliet's balcony scene, while
> I feel as if my own soul was on my lips, and my colour comes and goes with the intensity of the
> sentiment I am expressing: which prevents me from falling over my train, from setting fire to
> myself with the lamps placed close to me and from leaning upon my canvas balcony when I seem
> to throw myself all but over it (Archer, 1888/1957).

Indeed, far from being counter-productive, the 'watchful faculty' can enhance the
actor's creativity. This is what Stanislavsky's fictional student, Kostya, had to say on
the matter:

> As I was taking my bath I recalled the fact that while I was playing the part of the Critic I still
> did not lose the sense of being myself. The reason, I concluded, was that while I was acting I felt
> exceptionally pleased as I followed my own transformation. Actually I was my own observer at
> the same time that another part of me was being a fault-finding, critical creature. Yet can I really
> say that that creature is not a part of me? I derived him from my own nature. I divided myself, as
> it were, into two personalities. One continued as an actor, the other was an observer. Strangely
> enough this duality not only did not impede, it actually promoted my creative work. It encoura-
> ged and lent impetus to it (Stanislavski, 1977).

'Promoted my creative work'—this is the crucial point: divided consciousness does not 'impede' but is a boon to the actor's creativity. It is a point reiterated by actors time and time again. Over a period of five years, Russell-Parks interviewed eighty professional actors and fifty-six student actors from varying backgrounds about their experiences in performance. She concluded that all actors interviewed 'cited knowledge of a particular transformational experience known to take place in performance'. This 'transformational experience' was defined as 'some kind of significant alteration of the perceiving consciousness during performance'. The 'transformational experience' described by many of Russell-Parks' respondents was considered to be positive (Russell-Parks, 1989).

Interestingly, the actors she surveyed did 'not contemplate character or action or actor goals during performance'. Rather, all actors interviewed 'in the study felt that consciousness of their actor goals in terms of character inhibited a genuine performance'. Rather, all of the actors in performance thought about 'vocal effectiveness, appropriateness of physical gesture, audience reaction, consistency of facial gesture, critical responses to characterisation and self-evaluation'. This was, according to most of the actors interviewed, an alteration 'beyond becoming the character':

Tom Mull: 'It's not just being in character.'

Shelli Manzoline: 'I used to think it was. I think a lot of people think that it is. Especially the young actors around here. But then one night it takes off and that's it. You know that's what acting is. And it is some kind of step beyond being the character' (Russell-Parks, 1989).

Russell-Parks' findings are corroborated by Elly Konijn's survey of 114 professional stage actors. In performance, the majority of actors questioned experienced what Konijn refers to as 'task emotions' as opposed to 'character-emotions'. Task emotions relate to an actor's 'awareness of evaluative spectators with high expectations, in front of whom difficult acting tasks have to be performed' (Konijn, 1995).

What these actors describe is consistent with what sport psychologists have termed 'peak experiences'—those experiences that are associated with peak performance or what Chandler Atkins terms 'superior functioning' (Atkins, 1990). Peak experiences are 'transpersonal' (Privette, 1983), described as transcending 'the usual forms of consciousness' (Armor, 1969). They are characterized, among other things, by 'slowed passage of time', 'reduced fatigue/pain' and 'out of body sensations', 'detachment and control' (Atkins, 1990). In addition to this, these transpersonal, peak experiences are also considered a vital component of creative acts: 'the spice, the sense of adventure in the creative moment' (Blanchard, 1969).

Despite the overwhelming evidence of the occurrence and value of divided consciousness in performance, and its links to creativity, it is not a subject explicitly addressed in the curricula of acting schools. In my early training, I played Lady Torrance in Tennessee William's *Orpheus Descending*. One night—for the first time—I occasionally 'left my body' and was 'watching' myself play the part, almost guiding and coaching myself as I was acting on stage. After the performance I thought I had 'lost' it: that I must have given a terrible performance because I was not totally in character or 'in the moment'—that Holy Grail actors are taught to strive for. It came as a complete surprise to me when the director (not at all usually forthcoming with praise) congratulated me on a fine performance, but provided no answers to my questions: *'What happened to me out there, tonight? What was that all about?'* Russell-Parks observes that this 'experience seems part of every actor's consciousness. And yet no actor questioned on the subject could recall having discussed this aspect of acting in their acting classes' (Russell-Parks, 1989). The question remains: why?

There are many possible reasons: one could be that the concept of divided consciousness may seem somewhat mystical and not 'scientific' enough for those who share with Stanislavsky the desire to develop a systematic and objective training. Another reason could lie in the association of split consciousness with the madness of multiple personality. Actor George C. Scott commented in an interview:

> 'I think you have to be schizoid three different ways to be an actor. You've got to be three different people: you have to be a human being, then you have to be the character you're playing, and on top of that you've got to be the guy sitting out there in row 10, watching yourself and judging yourself. That's why most of us are crazy to start with or go nuts when we get into it' (Benedetti, 1990).

Russell-Parks gives yet another possible reason why divided consciousness is a neglected topic in actor training: she claims that it is due to 'a critical prejudice' which 'assigns the aesthetic experience to the audience' (and, one could add, the director) 'and not to the performer'. She counters, however, that the 'aesthetic experience is not restricted to the perspective of the art observer'. Citing Mikel Dufrenne: if 'this transcendence has a meaning, it exists first and foremost for the performer' (Russell-Parks, 1989).

Beyond all these reasons, in the hegemonic acting of psychological realism—defined primarily in terms of the actor's emotional identification with character—any 'distancing' or 'gap' between actor and character is to be avoided. Consequently, the concept of the actor's aesthetic perception or divided consciousness becomes pejorative. Not all of Archer's informants, for instance, welcomed the 'watchful faculty': some resented the suggestion of a divided consciousness 'as though it implied carelessness or unconscientiousness on their part'. Forbes Robertson, for example, perceived it as a sign that his 'work is getting mechanical' (Archer, 1888/1957). Other respondents replied, not surprisingly, 'that the actor should be 'absorbed' in his character'. Since the emergence of Naturalism and its psychologically 'real' characters, the notion of the actor's aesthetic distance in performance implies that they are not truly 'in the moment' or they are 'out of character'; it is evidence of a gap which the ideal acting seeks to close. This has led to polarization: if there is complete identification with character, then there cannot be detachment. It is constructed as an *either-or* situation.

However, one could reverse this proposition. In fact, Zeami had already done so centuries ago. The argument for detachment versus identification which has, since Diderot, preoccupied acting discourse in the West, was not an issue for Zeami, for whom it was not a question of *either* mask *or* face, but both—mask *and* face. Masakazu writes that 'Zeami did not see the mask and face as requiring a choice among alternatives' but instead 'he wanted the actor to unify the two while retaining a positive consciousness of their opposition' (Masakazu, 1984). Centuries later and worlds apart, Archer also concludes that it is not a question of masks or faces, but both: the actors he interviewed were 'almost unanimous in holding that presence of mind [...] by no means proves that the actor is personally unmoved' (Archer, 1888/1957). One century on, Russell-Parks' own survey of actors shows that there exists 'an abstracted mode of perception, in which the actor seems to exist within a simultaneously perceived and created aesthetic object' (Russell-Parks, 1989). In this latter mode of perception, the actor:

> may perceive herself gesturing in such a manner to note the audience reaction, and recognize a successful communication. She may do this without leaving character, or more to the point, without breaking the flow of her work on the stage. In another moment that actor may recognize the way in which a gelled light affects her skin tone or her costume, and physically adjust to take most advantage of the aesthetic affect she has perceived (Russell-Parks, 1989).

Given the widespread evidence of actors' divided consciousness in performance, Russell-Parks is right to claim that the 'needed directional change in actor-training' is 'a new kind of focus that will permit a highly receptive consciousness', not as a side-issue, but 'as the core of a stage discipline'.

There are those who have found in Asian martial arts and meditation practices inspiration for nurturing performance consciousness in actors. For example, in the late-1970s, enthused by the earlier training of A.C. Scott, Zarrilli established 'a repeatable set of intensive psychophysiological techniques' including 'breath control exercises, *t'ai chi ch'uan,* kalarippayatta, and selected yoga exercises' in order to cultivate the 'bodymind toward a state of readiness' (Zarrilli, 2002). Zarrilli defines this 'state of readiness' as 'an optimal condition for the actor', a condition which, in the words of Copeau, 'allows the artist...at the same time to be possessed by what he is expressing and to direct its expression' (Zarrilli, 2002). In *Psychophysical Acting*, Zarrilli explores among other things, how actors 'might better inhabit this paradoxical place of experience, awareness, and (double/multiple) consciousness' (Zarrilli, 2009).

It is this 'double/multiple' consciousness that *CREATICS* training aims to nurture in the actor. For it is in this state of divided consciousness that actors are able to successfully perform: to observe and direct themselves, to monitor the performance situation—including the audience—and to do all this without losing focus on what they are actually doing on stage.

Switch

Recently, a young student-actor confessed to me: *'Acting scares me. There is so much happening all at once and your mind has to be working 200% on so many levels'*. The good news is that with training, all this becomes second nature. The 'Brownies' of the mind become quite naturally part and parcel of what actors do out there in performance.

This exercise juggles the multiple points of attention the actor has in play in performance. Once again, it can be used in workshops or rehearsals.

1. The actors act out a scene they are working on with their attention focussed on realizing their fictional world: *'See it 'materialize' around you. Feel it. Is it hot, cold, stuffy, airy? Listen to the sounds in this world. Take in the smells...'*

2. The actors are then instructed to focus 100% on their character's objectives or tasks: *'Let the achieving of your objective or task preoccupy every part of you'* and *'If you hit obstacles, find new strategies.'*

3. Next, the actors are asked to focus their awareness onto their partner/s and allow themselves to totally respond to them: *'It is important that you don't anticipate, but react 100% to your partner.'*

4. The actors then imagine that the space between them is alive. Their aim is to work together to keep the space alive and energised. Wherever they move—far apart, close, turning their backs on each other—they must keep the space between them energised. When this is established, instruct them to now let the audience in on the space they are sharing with their partner/s and sense the presence of the audience: *'Enjoy drawing your audience into your private space.'*

5. The actors are then instructed to use only their peripheral vision and avoid staring fixedly at their partner or particular points in the space. *'As well as taking in your partner, take in the space in front of you. To your sides. Behind. Below and above. And the audience—all simultaneously.'*

6. The shift in focus now is back to the actor's imaginative world: *'As you act the scene, place your attention on what you are seeing in your mind's eye. What images spring to mind? Let them move you.'*

7. The actors now switch between these multiple objects of their attention: *'Shift your attention to what you are seeing in your mind's eye. Now, shift your attention 100% onto your partner. Now onto achieving your objective. Put your attention out into your audience. Imagine you are in the audience, watching what you are doing. Shift to taking in the space that surrounds you. Put your attention onto the time of day of your scene. Now focus on the air of your fictional world—is it stifling, close, refreshing, cold, bitter?'*

    I prompt the actors like this, switching not too rapidly, so that they have enough time to place their attention—and not too slowly so that they experience the exhilaration of switching their attention.

8. The actors finally juggle all the balls: instead of switching, they build their attention so that they are not focused on any one thing but try and work toward taking everything in. Rather than switching, when a new focus is introduced, they must add it to what they are already paying attention to.

Living Theatre's Julian Beck once asked: 'Why do you go to the theatre?' 'Do you', for example, 'go to the theatre to see how well an actor can disguise himself as somebody else?' Or 'do you go to the theatre for answers [...] to find out about life?' Maybe you 'go to the theatre for sexual stimulation [...] you like rubbing up against the person next to you?' (Beck, 1986). Beck's sometimes tongue-in-cheek tone should not obfuscate the seriousness of this question. Based on her own study of acting students, Leah Lowe observes that this is a question that most students would not have seriously contemplated. Instead, they 'view theatre-going as a chance to hone their craft by observing how others practice it' (Lowe, 2007). But by experiencing theatre as a spectator, students of acting might begin to learn what they will be expected to create in performances, and they are usually surprised to discover that, as audience members themselves, they already want more than characterisation. Some common student responses I get to the question are: 'I want a good story well told', 'tension, atmosphere', 'to feel something not only emotionally, but physically—I want goose-bumps', 'something that looks good, I want the actors to look good in the space', 'I want to go wow, I could never do that!' 'I want to see actors taking risks, sweating for me', '*I want to see actors with presence.*'

4.4 Creating Presence

If you've ever been moved by a performance, if you have a favourite actor, a favourite performance, then you'll recognize that the saying and the doing are far from describing the totality of that experience. The bit that is missing is like the gulf between gymnastics and dance, between scales and Chopin, between typing and poetry. What is that extra bit? All sorts of expressions are used to describe this ability or facility in the actor to communicate this intangible to audiences—'star quality', 'instinct' or even 'It' Actor John Derum (Seton, 2004).

If the bedrock for performing is divided consciousness, then the peaks are *Eureka moments*. These are those instances when an actor makes an audience gasp. It is, in the words of Stanislavsky, something you 'can never forget, it is the event of a lifetime'. It has 'the quality of the unexpected which startles, overwhelms, stuns':

> Something that lifts the spectator off the ground, sets him in a land where he has never walked, but which he recognizes easily through a sense of foreboding or conjecture. He does, however, see this unexpected thing face to face, and for the first time. It shakes, enthralls, and engulfs him (Stanislavski, 1977).

It is in such moments as these that no one asks the question: *'Are actors creative?'*

However, before the spectator is placed 'in a land where he [or she] has never walked', there is a vital, preliminary step. For Eureka moments or 'beautiful surprises' to occur, in any creative act, it is essential to *create the space for them*. Crystal Wood-ward observes this in her father's work as a Nobel-prize winning organic chemist:

> *Woodward created a space, an arena, in which beautiful surprises could arise.* [...] May be that he feels initially as though he had spontaneously found something. *But at the same time he has created the [...] context in which the spontaneous can arise.* There is a sense of fit, as though the found unexpectedly 'fits' into the created. [...] A sense of fit that can bring a feeling of aesthetic pleasure [my emphasis] (Woodward, 1989).

Similarly, good performers create spaces in which novelty can occur, *and in which their audiences engage.* Jacques Lecoq is unequivocal on the importance of this latter point: 'I always look for an actor who 'shines', who develops a space around himself in which the spectators are also present' (Lecoq, 2002). Effective actors open up gaps in which audiences are given license to join them as co-creators or, at the very least, conspirators breathing the same air. These *liminal spaces* are arguably the actor's greatest creation, because it is here that performances take place. Victor Turner used the terms *liminal* and *liminoid* to describe the transitional time and space—the thresh-olds—wherein all creative acts take place (Turner, 1982). This is also where perfor-mances occur. Theatrical performances, according to David George, 'do not occur on stage nor in the auditorium but in between the two: they are, in effect, exercises in the creation and occupation of thresholds' (George, 1999). It can be said, therefore, that *actors create performances*. They are the primary creators not only *in* but *of* perfor-mances—these unique events in time and place.

How then can actors create these spaces in which performances occur? They do this by *creating presence*. Presence, commonly conceived as the ultimate enigma of acting, is arguably the actor's most important creation.

Presence is often conceived as an 'indefinable' and 'intangible quality' which, according to Stanislavsky, is possessed by a few fortunate actors:

> There are certain actors who have only to step on the stage and the public is already enthralled by them... What is the basis of the fascination they exercise? It is an indefinable, intangible quality... (Stanislavski, 1963).

Presence belongs to those actors we cannot take our eyes off, who are riveting, who draw us in, are magnetic, charming, and charismatic. Defined as 'the (forceful) impression made by a performer on an audience', stage-presence is a highly desir-able and supposedly innate quality (*OED* 'Stage' *n*. Def. 14). In *An Actor's Handbook*, Stanislavsky writes that as 'I grow older and think about our art, I am inclined to believe that the highest gift that nature can give an actor is stage charm'. But even while acknowledging presence, Stanislavsky abdicated from defining, analyzing and, therefore, teaching it: you either have 'It' or you don't. But presence is more than just something you are born with or an 'added extra', a sheen or patina that 'value adds' to the performance. It is a much more profound and complex (or, conversely, a less mysterious and unfathomable) phenomenon than is routinely conceived.

In the first place, presence is not a quality or thing but, more accurately, an *act*, *occasion* or *event*. Presence is *social*: 'the fact or condition of being present; the state of being with or in the same place as a person or thing; attendance, company, society, or association' (*OED* 'Presence' *n*. Def. 2a). In performance, presence is the occasion when the actor and audience are fully and totally in communion, when they are both consumed by the moment, and are fully present together. George makes the point that presence is not 'only something which an actor achieves at the height of his craft', but also 'describes the audience's peak experience' (George, 1999). Most Asian theatre forms have similar terms which all describe something special, experienced simultaneously by actor and audience. In Balinese theatre, for example, *taksu* represents both the performer's presence, and 'also a moment in a performance when something special 'comes off' which affects the audience as much as the dancer' (George, 1991). In Kathakali, there is *bhangi*, and in Noh, the flower moment or *hana*, which implies both novelty and presence: '[f]lower, charm and novelty: all three of these partake of the same essence' (Zeami, 1984).

Presence is arguably the most significant *interaction* in theatre: it is moments like these that actors and audiences, alike, desire. These are moments when, for Eugenio Barba, 'the dilation of the actor's presence and the spectator's perception corresponds to a dilation of the *fabula,* the plot and its interweavings, the drama, the story or the situation represented' (Barba, Savarese & Gough, 1991). The present can become so dilated or expanded that it may even seem to incorporate the extraordinary, where other time-spaces appear immanent. *Taksu*, for example, is proof that the performer and the performance have connected with an 'unseen audience of deities' (George, 1991). In the *Raslila* plays of India, the performances serve to summon Krishna to be present. It is noteworthy that in one of its earliest uses in English, presence defines 'the manner in which Christ is held to be present in the Eucharist' (*OED* 'Presence' *n*. Def. 2c). This exclusive association with the Divine becomes more catholic in the seventeenth century, extending to any 'person or thing that exists or is present in a place but is not seen, *esp*. a divine, spiritual, or incorporeal being or influence felt or perceived to be present' (*OED* 'Presence' *n*. Def. 6). In a modern theatrical context, Australian director Simon Phillips observes:

> You see the actor connecting with something on a higher level, and they are able to play it in such a way that brings the heart up into the room in a kind of super-reality that is 'undeniable' and absolutely true to that moment (Macaulay, 2003).

If presence is an experience which stamps an actor or performer as truly creative, the crucial question remains whether one can train actors to achieve presence, or to be more present. One further etymological foray clears the path for this possibility. In the fifteenth century, presence was defined in terms of a personal attribute; it was used to denote 'a person's self or embodied personality' (*OED* 'Presence' *n.* Def. 4a). In the latter part of the sixteenth century a new definition expanded on that and, although it still links presence to notions of personality and selfhood, it is now also conceived that presence is a skill, a 'capacity' whose source is in actions, specifically in how one deports or carries themselves:

> Demeanour, carriage *esp.* when stately or impressive; nobleness or handsomeness of bearing or appearance, *esp.* the capacity to project or suggest inner strength, force of personality, etc., merely by being present (*OED* 'Presence' *n.* Def. 5a).

Presence is here recast as something which is *done, enacted,* or *performed*, and consequently it must be possible that presence can, to some extent, be acquired and taught.

From a Western perspective, where presence is commonly conceived of as an innate quality, and not an acquired ability, teaching presence may appear a radical proposition. In Stanislavsky's view, presence is outside of the actor's control—'an inner tidal wave', an 'unexpected something' which 'has surged up from the well springs of organic nature', enthralling, overwhelming and carrying the actor 'away to a point beyond his own consciousness' (Stanislavski, 1977).

Michael Chekhov, on the other hand, believed that presence could be cultivated. In *On The Technique of Acting*, he maintains that while some actors have natural presence, 'others need to spend a good deal of time "Radiating" in order to develop it'. Chekhov defines *radiating* as the 'ability to send out the invisible essence of whatever quality, emotion, or thought' that the actor intends and rates it as 'one of the strongest means of expression':

> On the stage the actor will feel himself as a kind of center that continuously expands in any and all directions he chooses. More than this, the actor will be able, *through the power of Radiation*, to convey to the audience the finest and most subtle nuances of his acting, and the deepest meaning of the text and situations. In other words, the audience will receive the contents of the scenic moment together with the actor's most intimate and individual interpretation of it [my emphasis] (Chekhov, 1991).

Although Chekhov believed that 'Radiation' could come of itself, he argued that it was possible to achieve a radiating presence 'through exercises' which he outlines in some detail in *On The Technique of Acting*.

Booth

The following is a simple, yet effective warm-up for achieving presence.

1. The actors find their own space and imagine they are standing in a glass booth.

2. They make contact with all surfaces of the booth with as many parts of their body as possible—and not just their hands! '*Feel the glass with your hips, backs of your legs, belly, buttocks... Leave your body prints on the glass.*'

3. They are now told that the booth is shrinking: '*As the booth gets smaller, feel which parts of your body come into contact with the glass.*'

4. After the booth has become as small as possible instruct the actors to feel all the parts of their body which are in contact with the glass: '*Be aware of how your body is filling this tiny space. Where is your left leg? The base of your spine? The back of your neck? Breathe into all these body parts as you identify them. While you are crammed into this tight space, fill it up with your body and breath. Feel big. Be enormous in this tiny space. And although your body is restricted, your energy is strong—at 100%.*'

5. Now the booth will gradually expand: '*Feel how each part of your body touching the glass now loses contact and bit by bit the body slowly releases into the expanding space. As you expand, don't lose the energy you had in the small space. Breathe into the different parts of your body as they unfurl.*'

6. The booth expands to the point where it shatters and the actors are free to move in the space, while maintaining the energy they achieved in the booth.

7. Finally, the actors return to their booths and, standing in neutral position, they feel as if they are filling their booth—allowing their bodily presence to fill the space: '*When I clap my hands, the booth will once again shatter and you will be standing in the open space, but without losing the energy you achieved in the booth.*' The actors stand and then move in the space feeling their full presence.

A cursory survey of some Asian theatrical traditions reveals not only extensive theorizing on presence, but also specific strategies, techniques and methods for achieving it which, it must be stressed, need not remain restricted to this source. Notwithstanding that the source of presence is, according to Zeami, elusive (precisely where can it be located?' he asks. 'It seems to be found nowhere') he does not underestimate the role of skill in its achievement. Zeami articulates how actors can create and maximize presence in a way which is quite startlingly simple, teachable and learnable: actors can fascinate audiences if, for example, they juxtapose body and feet movements—'Violent Body Movement, Gentle Foot Movements'—or if they communicate to audiences 'first by hearing and then by sight':

> in the matter of weeping the actor should first allow the audience to hear the word 'weeping', and then, just afterwards, bring the sleeve up to the face and so complete the total action with this gesture. If the audience sees the motion of the sleeve before the concept of weeping is settled

in their minds, however, the words will somehow seem left over. [...] The total image will lack intensity (Zeami, 1984).

In addition to these techniques, there is the skill of 'mutuality of balance', namely countering freedom of movement with the control of *jo, ha, kyu* (Zeami, 1984). If this is achieved, then the flower will bloom and presence will be achieved.[1]

For the Chinese *jingju* (Peking or Beijing Opera) performer, presence is similarly vital. Jo Riley stresses that the *jingju* actor 'must *fa qi* (radiate presence)', because if not 'the performance is considered worthless, a waste of effort' (Riley, 1997). *Qi* simultaneously represents some sort of divine inspiration and, more prosaically, 'breath control'. The *jingju* actor is trained, therefore, to 'ensure he has the right quantity of breath [*qi* or presence] at all times'. Riley observes that in 'training, the master will often point to the student's abdomen and demand that the student draw up his *qi*'. In addition to this, the set poses of *jingju* are designed to retain *qi* and not dissipate it. In fact, the entire *jingju* performance is itself structured around maximizing the actor's presence or *qi*. Riley makes the point that the 'performer moves on the stage curving around one point, and moving directly to another, like a chess piece on a board. As he does so, he is involved in a process of continual expending and gathering of qi' (Riley, 1997).

These techniques belong to highly codified traditions, very different to Western theatre forms, especially the theatre of psychological realism. However, Eugenio Barba's research into theatre anthropology has shown that there are certain, specific, underlying principles which are common to a broad cross-section of Asian performance traditions—and which can also be identified in Western praxes. All of these serve one thing: presence. It is perhaps Barba, above all, in Western actor training, who has paved the way for training for presence. In fact, as Ian Watson notes, Barba's 'analysis of presence [...] and how to control it technically are the essence of his acting theory' (Watson, 1993). In Barba's own words:

> I am interested in a very, very elemental question. Why when I see two actors on stage doing the same thing, I get fascinated by one and not by the other? (Barba, 1984).

As a first step towards answering this question, Barba distinguishes between what he calls 'extra-daily' and 'daily' techniques.[2] Daily techniques refer to the 'way we use our bodies in daily life' which, according to Barba, 'is substantially different from

---

1 Rimer and Masakazu suggest that *jo, ha, kyu* can be literally translated as 'introduction' (*jo*), 'breaking' (*ha*), and 'rapid' (*kyu*) (Zeami, 1984). According to Dymphna Callery, at the macro-scale, *jo, ha, kyu* refers to 'the overall flow of a play', and on the 'micro-scale' to the 'interior qualitative dynamic of each move and utterance' (Callery, 2001).

2 Barba also defines a third category: 'techniques of virtuosity'. Used in acrobatics, for example, these techniques 'aim for amazement and the transformation of the body' (Barba, Savarese & Gough, 1991).

the way we use them in performance' (Barba, Savarese & Gough, 1991). In performance, Barba claims that extra-daily techniques are required. Distinct from, but not completely separate from daily techniques, 'they maintain a tension between them without becoming isolated' (Barba, Savarese & Gough, 1991). The actor's actions and gestures are neither necessarily discernible nor obviously distinct from everyday behaviour but, Barba argues, spectators are drawn in, because by utilizing these extra-daily techniques the actor achieves 'scenic bios', 'biological presence' or 'scenic presence'.

One of the frequent challenges in teaching young actors or actors coming from TV or film is getting them to come to terms with the kind of energy and presence stage performance requires. Influenced by a style of acting they commonly see or encounter on TV or in films, they tend to value what they perceive as 'natural' and eschew the 'theatrical'. I find, more often than not, that they view being relaxed and comfortable on stage as their goal and that anything that goes beyond this is considered 'hammy' or 'over-the-top'. It takes a while and some experience performing on stage for them to grasp that acting in theatrical performances is not like behaving as if at home or on the street. Michael Chekhov makes the point:

> The actor feels himself so comfortable, so irresponsibly at ease on the stage, he swims in coziness and even in danger of becoming languid. He is acting just as though he were at home (Chekhov, 1991).

Inflation!

This exercise helps actors embody and endow their characters with heightened presence in the space, while simultaneously ensuring that they remain connected to the source of the character's energy.

1. Without actually moving, the actors begin adjusting their bodies to take on the shape of their character, to embody the image they see in their imagination.
2. After a clap of the hands, they instantly embody the image, collapse into it, and begin to move through the space. They are coached to become aware of which part of the body their character leads with—and then encouraged to experiment with different ways of walking and observe what differences this might make to their character: '*Lead with your forehead, pelvis, left knee...*'
3. The actors then move as if their characters are heavy, light, fast, slow—and play with these variables, once again noting how the different weights and tempos affect their characters.
4. As the actors move through the space, they imagine that their characters are like inflatable dolls—gradually expanding in energy and filling the space until they feel they have come to the point of bursting. Then, standing still and totally inflated, they speak their characters' names—'*I am Electra*'—as if to the ceiling, to the air in front of them, the space behind, the floor, the audience.

5. Moving through the space again, the actors allow their characters to gradually deflate until they completely collapse and all that is alive is a little flicker inside of them, a flickering flame. In the quiet of this collapsed state, they locate this energy, this flame, this flicker—this is the source of their character's energy, their wants desires, loves and hates: *'No matter how inflated your character is, how full its presence is in the space—you are always connected to this flicker'*.

6. In this collapsed state with their attention on their energy source, the actors whisper what their characters love, hate and want more than anything in the world. Alternating between these 3 utterances, they fuel their energy until they start to inflate first to standing, then moving and finally, filling the space again.

7. Finally, the actors now explore a repertoire of movements: *'How does your character stand, sit in a chair and get up? What gestures does your character make? Experiment with the gesture, ensuring it is clear with a definite beginning middle and end.'* They perform this repertoire of movements with an 'inflated' sense of their bodies in the space—whilst never letting the inner flame extinguish.

It can be argued that in spite of his doubts regarding whether presence can be taught or even acquired, Stanislavsky was concerned with 'immediacy and presence on stage', his System aiming at achieving 'a sense of being fully present in the dramatic moment' (Carnicke, 1998). Certainly, concepts such as character objectives, absorption and concentration, faith and focus can all be conceived of as techniques of presence. However, they differ from Barba's techniques in one crucial way: Stanislavsky's concept of presence is hitched to a fictive character, whereas Barba's is linked to the actor's 'pre-expressive' body. In *A Dictionary of Theatre Anthropology,* he writes:

> In the Occidental tradition, the performer's work has been oriented towards a network of fictions, of 'magic ifs' which deal with the psychology, the behaviour and the history of his or her person and that of the character he or she is playing. The pre-expressive principles of the performer's life are not cold concepts concerned only with the body's physiology and mechanics. They also are based on a network of fictions, but fictions, 'magic-ifs', which deal with the physical forces which move the body. What the performer is looking for, in this case, is a fictive body, not a fictive personality (Barba, Savarese & Gough, 1991).

Drawing from a diverse range of Western and non-Western performance traditions, Barba identifies three 'pre-expressive' principles—*precarious balance, opposition and omission*— which are common to all. In *CREATICS*, I have translated these principles into acting exercises. They provide a scaffolding on which training for presence can be built.

The first principle—*precarious balance*—defines 'the abandonment of daily balance in favour of a "precarious" or extra-daily "balance"' (Barba, Savarese & Gough, 1991). It is this 'dynamic balance, based on the body's tensions' that has the potential to arouse an audience's kinaesthetic responses and generate 'the sensation of movement in the spectator even when there is only immobility' (Barba, Savarese & Gough, 1991). Through precarious balance, the performer can create presence 'at a stage which precedes intentional, individualised expression' (Barba, Savarese & Gough, 1991). It is, according to Barba, the 'characteristic most common to actors and dancers from different cultures and times' (Barba, Savarese & Gough, 1991). Examples of precarious balance can be found in the serpentine *tribhangi* posture of traditional Indian dance, the animated poses of *commedia dell'arte* actors, and the twentieth-century mime tradition of Étienne Decroux.

Precarious balance need not, however, be restricted to physically stylized genres. The principle of the body in disequilibrium is just as useful for the actor working in psychological realism. In this context, the balance is likely to be less precarious, but it could, nevertheless, usefully inform the actor's physicality, making the actor appear more dynamic. This runs counter to a rather widespread notion in contemporary Western training that the actor should be in equilibrium. Jean Benedetti, for example, claims that actors 'need a firm sense of balance and the ability to transfer weight without losing control or equilibrium' (Benedetti, 1998). However, this is to ignore the energy that precarious balance can bestow on an actor. Rudolf Arnheim makes the point that 'movement looks dead when it gives the impression of mere displacement', or what Benedetti refers to as the 'ability to transfer weight without losing control' (Barba, Savarese & Gough, 1991). On the contrary, movement looks alive, even in moments of immobility, when the body is neither always in balance nor is fully at ease as Stanislavsky's Tortsov advocates in *An Actor Prepares*, exhorting the students to '[r]elax more!'. While on stage, he argues, the actor must 'feel more at ease than when you are at home'. Yet such a state of relaxation in an actor is clearly not desirable, and one suspects that Stanislavsky thought as much too. Barba makes the point that the 'impulse to action' which 'alters balance and breaks the body line' (what the Odin Teatret termed '*sats*') is similar to Stanislavsky's notion of 'standing in the right rhythm'. Barba cites an anecdote from Toporkov's *Stanislavski in Rehearsal,* where Stanislavsky suggests that an actor stand as if watching for a mouse around the corner: 'Do you feel the difference?' he asks 'To stand and watch for a mouse—that is one rhythm: to watch a tiger that is creeping up on you is quite another' (Barba, Savarese & Gough, 1991).

Rather than striving for balance, comfort, or ease, actors should work toward what Decroux calls being 'at ease in unease' (Barba, Savarese & Gough, 1991). Actors should be encouraged to take risks and exit the comfort of what Bogart and Landau term the 'Gray Zone' (Bogart & Landau, 2005). It is then actors are more likely to engage and excite their audience.

Knots

In this exercise, the actors work in pairs and then groups to form a knot with their bodies. The knot is mobile, so they must be able to move through the space. The aim is to develop a sense of being at ease in precarious balance.

1. Working in pairs, the actors get into the tightest knot possible.
2. They then establish their centre: *'Find the point where you are most strongly connected. Don't discuss it. Come to an agreement about where your shared centre is without talking.'*
3. The pairs now move through the space maintaining their knot. At first, they are instructed to move together in the same direction, and then told to move in opposite directions, while keeping attached and their centre strong. Then they are urged to follow their impulses: *'You can change between moving in the same direction as each other or in the opposite direction.'*
4. Moving through the space the pairs now attach to another pair to form a new knot with a new centre. Once again, *'Find the point where you are most strongly connected. Don't talk about it. Come to an agreement about where your shared centre is without talking.'*
5. In the next stage, things get a little more aggressive: *'Moving through the space as this bigger knot, your aim as a group is to take over another group while avoiding being taken over. Throughout this you must keep your knot in tact. Do not lose contact with the others despite how precarious your balance might be. Maintain your centre, no matter how far you might move away from it.'*
6. Each time a new group is formed a new knot and centre is established.
7. This continues until there is one group with one centre or one group manages to avoid being taken over.

Knots can be adapted to scene work. As the actors play the scene, they are given license to physically attach to their acting partner(s) when they have the impulse to do so. However, there is a catch. Once attached, no matter how much they might want to get away, they cannot. They can only break contact if they have an exit in the scene, but otherwise, they can only move as far from their acting partner(s) as is physically possible without breaking the 'knot'. Finally, the actors play the scene unattached, while physically maintaining the *precarious balance* they were forced into when 'knotted' together.

In this activity, actors experience, in a very physical sense, the push and pull between their characters—the drawing together and forcing apart which puts them off balance.

Victor Turner's description of liminality could equally pertain to the thrill of watching an actor in precarious balance: 'the past is momentarily negated, suspended, or abrogated, and the future has not yet begun, an instant of pure potentiality when everything, as it were, trembles in the balance' (Turner, 1982). It is also a fitting description for creativity as such, because precarious balance—what Koestler describes as the 'transitory state of unstable equilibrium'—is a characteristic of all creative acts (Koestler, 1970).

Barba's second principle of pre-expressivity—*opposition*—is one means to facilitate precarious balance, but is also more than that. Barba claims that the 'performer's body reveals its life to the spectator by means of a tension between opposing forces' (Barba, Savarese & Gough, 1991). This principle also has a long history: creating oppositions and juxtapositions was crucial, for instance, to Zeami's actor. Masakazu makes the point that Zeami's theory of acting was, to a great degree, based on the premise that 'man's sensitivity is heightened by the addition of an opposing element' (Masakazu, 1984). From this principle, Zeami developed several techniques and strategies, notably: appearing 'angry while possessing a tender heart' and moving 'in a powerful way' while stamping the feet 'in a gentle way':

> To appear angry while possessing a tender heart gives rise to the principle of novelty. On the other hand, in a performance requiring Grace, an actor must not forget to remain strong. [...] When he moves himself about in a powerful way, he must stamp his foot in a gentle way. And when he stamps his feet strongly, he must hold the upper part of his body quiet (Zeami, 1984).

The principle of opposition informs many aspects of Noh, including the basic Noh walk, where actors walk forward as if somebody is pulling them back by their hips. This creates *koshi* or energy, as does the basic Noh posture, where the 'actor must imagine that above him is suspended a ring of iron which is pulling him upwards' and 'must resist this pull in order to keep his feet on the ground' (Barba, Savarese & Gough, 1991). This opposition between the head and feet is one that is commonplace in Western training, where it is recognized that this tension creates an energized body. In Viewpoints training, for example, warm-ups include standing, walking or running while imagining 'a golden band around your head pulling gently upward', 'bare feet accustomed to working in the soil' and 'an open heart'. All these opposing images work toward 'a line between heaven and earth' and energizing the body when it becomes 'exhausted or confused' (Bogart & Landau, 2005).

For the same reason, it is just as important in performance. Like precarious balance, oppositions in the body generate an energy which, in the words of Barba, creates a 'kind of *elementary drama*', which is 'sensed kinaesthetically by the spectator as a conflict between elementary forces' (Barba, Savarese & Gough, 1991). This tension between opposing forces can usefully inform the playing of a scene and enrich the complexity of a role. Zeami recognized this when he advised actors playing the role of the old man, for instance, that they should 'resemble an old tree' but one that still 'puts forth flowers' (Zeami, 1984).

Impulse / Repulse

I use Barba's pre-expressive principle of opposition in the following exercise to steer actors away from their impulses. Of course, following their instincts or impulses is important for actors (or any artist, for that matter), but it can be liberating, at times, not to. So often when actors are told to follow their impulses, they think they are entering unchartered territory but, in fact, they are often following their impulses to be in a safe place and respond in a way that is comfortable and familiar to them. However, in going against the grain and repulsing their impulses, they often enter new territories.

1. The actors walk the space: *'Feel yourself expand into the space and devour the space with your body. Follow your instincts. Move wherever you want to move and however you want to move— forwards, backwards, sideways, upright, close to the ground, quickly or slowly, moving towards people or away from them. All the time, just follow your instincts.'*
2. Then they are instructed NOT to follow their instincts: *'If you want to move right, don't—move left. If you want to move slowly, go fast. If you are attracted by something move away from it.'*
3. They now return to following their impulses.
4. Next, they switch between the two: *'When I call out repulse—do not follow your instincts, and when I call out impulse—follow your instincts.'*
5. Finally, they are invited to *repulse* or *impulse* at will.

This exercise can be used in rehearsals to jolt actors out of the predictable. A director can coach actors to repulse: *'You stormed towards Don Juan, shouting, your hand ready to hit him. Don't follow your instincts now. Oppose them. Fight them. See what happens'*. What can happen is something startling, surprising, stunning.

Taking a broader perspective for a moment, just as precarious balance may be considered a trait of all creative acts, so too can opposition and juxtaposition. Koestler describes the creative act as 'bisociative', meaning by this that it involves the interaction between 'two independent matrices of perception or reasoning' (Koestler, 1970). The greater the difference between the matrices, the greater the creative impact. Koestler's conception of creativity as 'connecting previously unrelated dimensions of experience' is consistent with how some eminent creators have described their own practices. Mathematician Henri Poincaré, for example, described creativity in mathematics as making combinations 'which reveal to us unsuspected kinship between other facts, long known, but wrongly believed to be strangers to one another' (Ghiselin, 1952). These 'unsuspected kinships' cannot occur, in the words of Anne Bogart and Tina Landau: 'if one is always looking for a particular premeditated result'. If this is the case, then many things that are happening outside of those parameters are not recognized' (Bogart & Lindau, 2005). This, of course, is the big drawback of Stanislavsky's methodology. William Worthen makes the point that while preparing the actor for 'artistic acting', Stanislavsky's methodology is 'an implicit restriction as well', because the 'actor is urged to embody a deterministic model of character that is fundamentally at odds with the autonomous performance he attempts to create onstage' (Worthen, 1983).

Omission, the third and last of Barba's pre-expressive principles, similarly facilitates presence and can be argued to inform all creative acts. Barba defines it as 'the omission of certain elements in order to put other elements into relief', making them appear 'essential' (Barba, Savarese & Gough, 1991). This is achieved on stage by eliminating all the fussiness of everyday movements, refining them to what is essential both expressively and aesthetically. It also refers to the concentration of the performer's energy, namely, the 'compression, into restricted movements, of the same energy which would be used to accomplish a much larger and heavier action' (Barba, Savarese & Gough, 1991). Once again, Zeami is apposite: the principle of omission is encapsulated in his instruction 'when you feel ten in your heart, express seven in your movements'. Zeami writes:

> In terms of general stage deportment, no matter how slight a bodily action, if the motion is more restrained than the emotion behind it, the emotion will become the Substance and the movements of the body its Function, thus moving the audience (Zeami, 1984).

Anne Bogart invokes Zeami when she observes that a 'great actor, like a striptease artist, withholds more than she or he shows'. Like Zeami, she maintains that this 'concentration and restraint generate energy in the actor and interest in the audience'. She goes on to say:

> An actor's special gift is the ability to resist, to hold back, to tame, to keep energy in, to concentrate. With this compression, the actor plays with the spectators' kinesthetic sensibilities (Bogart, 2001).

The same point was made by Tyrone Guthrie who, when asked 'Surely actors are just showing off?' replied, 'On the contrary... what they are doing is hiding' (Szeps, 1996). The actor's creativity always lies in choosing what to show and, more importantly, what to hide.

7/10

The name of this exercise is taken from Zeami's instruction to actors: 'when you feel ten in your heart, express seven in your movements'.

1. A scene where the stakes are high is chosen. Or alternatively actors in pairs improvise a scene, based on an opening line which lends itself to confrontation (e.g. *Why did you do that? Why did you come back? Where were you last night? Do you really believe that?*).

2. There are two rules:
- One of the actors must attempt to leave at some point in the scene
- The scene must occur in a private place
3. The actors first improvise the scene without discussing given circumstances. They are reminded that the stakes are high: *'This is "life" or "death". All or nothing!'*
4. They then sketch out some Given Circumstances: *'who are you?', 'What is your relationship?', 'Where are you?', ' What has just happened?'*
5. The actors keep working the scene, refining it so that the lines are set. It is important they are reminded of the stakes and urged towards a very emotionally charged scene with no holds barred.
6. Once the actors have reached a point where they are at the limit and 'exploding' in the scene, get them to stop and now: *'Play the scene as if you are in a crowded lift. Although you are constrained by being in this tiny, public space, the intensity is still at the 100% you found in your private space. How does it feel in your body? Where do you feel the tension? Where do you feel the 'bubbling' inside you? What are you doing to keep a lid on things?'*
7. Now the actors return to their private space and: *'Play the scene with the lid on.* They are reminded: *'Concealing and containing your emotions does not mean that there is not a volcano inside you waiting to erupt.'*
8. You may need to go back to the public (letting it all hang out) improvisation a couple of times, so that the actors don't lose touch with the energy they found there.

As is the case with precarious balance and opposition, omission is also an important aspect of all creative acts. Of Koestler's three main criteria of creativity: 'unexpectedness', 'emphasis', and 'economy' the last two relate to the principle of omission. According to Koestler, 'emphasis' refers to the process of choosing the relevant stimuli and omitting 'non-essential elements' (Koestler, 1970). The chosen elements are then emphasized, exaggerated, or to use Barba's words 'put into relief'. 'Economy' is its counterbalance: where emphasis exaggerates, economy implies. Koestler describes it as 'hints instead of statements'. Economy tempers emphasis, ensuring that what is emphasized also remains, simultaneously, seductive to the receiver, in the way that Bogart's 'great actor' teases.

Tease!

1. Working individually in the space, preferably with their eyes closed, the actors are asked to recall some good or bad news they have received.
2. They are prompted to remember the moments just before they received the news: *'See these moments in your mind's eye. Feel them on your skin. In your body. Where were you? What was it like? What time of day? Sounds, smells...?'*

3. Remaining with their eyes closed and standing still, instruct the actors to receive the news: *'as if it is dripping into the top of your head, very slowly. Feel how the news spreads throughout your body, like coloured dye seeping in. Stay still throughout this, letting the news sink in.'*

4. Next, they are asked to locate where the news impacts the most: *'which part of your body does it hit? Put your attention here and to let it build, slowly and steadily until you cannot contain it any longer and it erupts in a single gesture.'*

5. Once they have let the gesture 'out', they work on refining it: *'establish its beginning, middle and end point'* (its jo ha kyu, if you like). Their gestures can be highly stylised or quite 'natural' and everyday, as long as they are definite and precise.

6. Now with their gesture worked out, the actors return to Steps, 2, 3 and 4. But this time, when they erupt, it is manifested in their refined gesture.

Presence can be defined, analyzed and facilitated. For in the end:

> What makes a Jeremy Irons 'interesting' is the same thing that draws the spectator to Panigrahi: a way of using the body, of moving through space, of gesturing, speaking, and making contact separate and prior to any 'characterisation' (Schechner, 1993).

It has been my ambition to help actors, their directors and teachers achieve this capacity to be 'interesting' in performance—to draw and engage their audiences. Performance is not just the end point of a process, the presentation of a prior creation. It is a new act of creation, for which both the text and the achievements made in rehearsal are merely a blueprint. In performance, actors must do more than act and it is this recognition of the expansive scope of the actor's creativity which has provided the rationale for this book and *CREATICS* training.

References

Albright, H., & Albright, A. (1980). *Acting: the creative process*. 3rd ed. Belmont CA: Wadsworth.

Amabile, T.M. (1983). *The Social Psychology of Creativity*. New York: Springer-Verlag.

Archer, W. (1957). *Masks or Faces?: a study in the psychology of acting*. New York: Hill & Wang. (Original work published in 1888)

Armor, T.A. (1969). Note on Peak Experience and Transpersonal Psychology. *Journal of Transpersonal Psychology 1*, 47-50.

Arnold, M. (1968). The Function of Criticism at the Present Time. In S. T. M. Hoctor (Ed.), *Essays in Criticism: First Series*. (pp. 8-30). Chicago & London: University of Chicago Press. (Original work published in 1865)

Arnold, N. (1991). The manipulation of the audience by director and actor. In G. D. Wilson (Ed.), *Psychology and Performing Arts*. (pp. 75-81). Amsterdam: Swets & Zeitlinger.

Atkins, C.W. (1990). *A comparative analysis of peak experience performance and non-peak experience performance in professional actors and actresses*. United States International University, San Diego.

Auslander, P. (1985). Task and Vision: Willem Dafoe in *L.S.D. The Drama Review, 29* (2), 94-98.

Baldwin, J. (2003). *Michel Saint-Denis and the Shaping of the Modern Actor*. Westport & London: Praeger.

Barba, E. (1984). Anthropology and Theatre: Interviews. *Performing Arts Journal 8* (3), 7-27.

Barba, E., Savarese, N., & Gough, R. (Eds.). (1991). *A Dictionary of Theatre Anthropology: The Secret Art of the Performer*. London & New York: Routledge.

Barish, J.A. (1981). *The Antitheatrical Prejudice*. Berkeley & New York: University of California Press.

Barthes, R. (1984). The Death of the Author. In *Image-Music-Text*. (pp. 142-148). London: Flamingo.

Barzun, J. (1991). The Paradoxes of Creativity. In H. Wilmer (Ed.), *Creativity: Paradoxes and Reflections*. (pp. 3-16). Wilmette: Chiron.

Beck, J. (1986). *The Life of the Theatre: the relation of the artist to the struggle of the people*. San Francisco: Limelight Editions.

Belfiore, E.S. (1992). *Tragic Pleasures: Aristotle on plot and emotion*. Princeton: Princeton University Press.

Benedetti, J. (1998). *Stanislavski and the Actor*. New York: Routledge/Theatre Arts.

Benedetti, R.L. (1990). *The Actor at Work*. 5th ed. Prentice Hall: New Jersey.

Bennett, S. (1997). *Theatre Audiences: a theory of production and reception*. 2nd ed. London & New York: Routledge.

Bishop, C.A. (1988). *The deconstructed actor: towards a postmodern acting theory*. University of Colorado, Boulder.

Blanchard, W.H. (1969). Psychodynamic aspects of peak experience. *Psychoanalytic Review 84*, 191-215.

Boden, M.A. (1999). Computer Models of Creativity. In R. J. Sternberg (Ed.), *Handbook of Creativity*. (pp. 351-372). Cambridge: Cambridge University Press.

—. (2004). *The Creative Mind: myths and mechanisms*. 2nd ed. London: Routledge.

Bogart, A. (2001). *A Director Prepares*. London & New York: Routledge.

Bogart, A., & Landau, T. (2005). *The Viewpoints Book: A Practical Guide to Viewpoints and Composition*. New York: Theatre Communications Group.

Brandon, J.R. (1989). A New World: Asian Theatre in the West Today. *The Drama Review, 33* (2), 25-50.

Bristol Old Vic Theatre School. (n.d.). 3rd year BA Professional Acting. In *Bristol Old Vic Theatre School* (para. 2). Retrieved March 7, 2014, from http://web.archive.org/web/20080103054149/ http://www.oldvic.ac.uk/3yr_ba_acting.html

Brown, S. (1996). *Bristol Old Vic Theatre School: the first 50 years 1946-1996*. Bristol: BOVTS Productions.

Burns, E. (1990). *Character: Acting and Being on the Pre-Modern Stage*. Basingstoke & London: Macmillan.

Callery, D. (2001). *Through the Body: a practical guide to physical theatre*. London: Nick Hern.

Caractère. (1992). In *Dictionnaire Historique de la Langue Française*.

Carlson, M. (1996). *Performance: a critical introduction*. London & New York: Routledge.

—. (1984). *Theories of the Theatre: A Historical and Critical Survey, from the Greeks to the Present*. Ithaca & London: Cornell University Press.

Carnicke, S.M. (1998). *Stanislavsky in Focus*. Amsterdam: Harwood Academic.

—. (2000). Stanislavsky's System: pathways for the actor. In A. Hodge (Ed.), *Twentieth Century Actor Training*. (pp. 11-36). London & New York: Routledge.

Casati, R. & Achille V. Events. (2006, May 8). In E.N Zalta (Ed.), *The Stanford Encyclopedia of Philosophy*. Retrieved October 3, 2007 from http://plato.stanford.edu/entries/events/

Chamberlain, F. (2010). Michael Chekhov on the Technique of Acting: 'Was Don Quixote True to Life?' In A. Hodge (Ed.), *Actor Training*. (pp. 63-80). London & New York: Routledge.

Chang, G.C.C. (1971). *The Buddhist teaching of Totality: the philosophy of Hwa Yen Buddhism*. Philadelphia: Penn State University Press.

Chekhov, M. (1991). *On the Technique of Acting*. New York: HarperPerennial.

Cole, T., & Chinoy, H.K. (Eds.). (1970). *Actors on Acting*. New York: Crown Publishers.

Coleridge, S.T. (1971). On the Slave Trade. In L. Patton & P. Mann (Eds.), *Lectures 1795 on Politics and Religion*. (pp. 231-252). London: Routledge & Kegan. (Original work published in 1795)

Crohn Schmitt, N. (1990). Theorizing about Performance: Why Now? *New Theatre Quarterly, 6* (23), 231-234.

Cruciani, F. (1991). Apprenticeship: Occidental Examples. In E. Barba, N. Savarese & R. Gough (Eds.), *A Dictionary of Theatre Anthropology: The Secret Art of the Performer*. (pp.26-29). London & New York: Routledge.

Csikszentmihalyi, M. (1999). Implications of a Systems Perspective for the Study of Creativity. In R.J. Sternberg (Ed.), *Handbook of Creativity*. (pp. 313-335). Cambridge: Cambridge University Press.

Dayan, D., & Katz, E. (1994). *Media Events: the live broadcasting of history*. Harvard: Harvard University Press.

Delgado, R. (1988). *Acting with Both Sides of Your Brain: perspectives on the creative process*. New York: Holt, Rinehart & Winston.

Diderot, D. (1922). *Paradoxe sur le Comédien*. Cambridge: Cambridge University Press. (Original work published 1830)

—. (1957). *The Paradox of Acting*. (W. H. Pollock, Trans.). New York: Hill & Wang. (Original work published 1830)

Donnellan, D. (2002). *The Actor and the Target*. London: Nick Hern.

Dufrenne, M. (1973). *The Phenomenology of the Aesthetic Experience*. Evanston: Northwestern University Press.

Else, G.F. (1957). *Aristotle's Poetics: The Argument*. Cambridge: Harvard University Press.

Endsley, M. (2006). Expertise and Situation Awareness. In K. Anders, N. Charness, P.J. Feltovich & R.R. Hoffman (Eds.), *The Cambridge Handbook of Expertise and Expert Performance*. (pp.633-652). Cambridge: Cambridge University Press.

Feist, G.J. (1999). The Influence of Personality on Artistic and Scientific Creativity. In R.J. Sternberg (Ed.), *Handbook of Creativity*. (pp. 273-296). Cambridge: Cambridge University Press.

Fenichel, O. (1960). On Acting. *The Tulane Drama Review, 4* (3), 148-159.

Gardner, H. (1993). *Creating Minds*. New York: Basic Books.

—. (1994). The Creator's Patterns. In M. Boden (Ed.), *Dimensions of Creativity*. (pp. 143-158). Cambridge, Mass. & London: MIT Press.

George, D.E.R. (1991). *Balinese Ritual Theatre*. Cambridge & Alexandria, VA: Chadwyck-Healey.

—. (1999) *Buddhism as/in Performance*. New Delhi: DK Printworld.

Ghiselin, B. (Ed.). (1952). *The Creative Process*. New York & Toronto: Mentor.

Grotowski, J. (2002). Towards a Poor Theatre. In E. Barba (Ed.), *Towards a Poor Theatre*. (pp. 15-25). New York: Routledge.

Grotowski, J., & Barba, E. (2002). The Theatre's New Testament. In E. Barba (Ed.), *Towards a Poor Theatre*. (pp. 27-53). New York: Routledge.

Gruber, H.E. (1989). The Evolving Systems Approach to Creative Work. In D B. Wallace & H.E. Gruber (Eds.), *Creative people at work: twelve cognitive case studies*. (pp. 2-24). New York: Oxford University Press.

Hausman, C.R. (1984). *A Discourse on Novelty and Creation*. Albany: State University New York Press.

Hilgard, E.E. (1986). *Divided Consciousness: Multiple Controls in Human Thought and Action*. New York: John Wiley & Sons.

Hope Mason, J. (2003). *The Value of Creativity: an essay on intellectual history, from Genesis to Nietzsche*. Aldershot: Ashgate.

Hornby, R. (2007). Feeding the System: the Paradox of the Charismatic Acting Teacher. *New Theatre Quarterly 23* (1), 67-72.

—. (1992). *The End of Acting: A Radical View*. New York: Applause Books.

Ingold, T., & Hallum, E. (2007). Creativity and Cultural Improvisation: An Introduction. In T. Ingold & E. Hallum (Eds.), *Creativity and Cultural Improvisation*. (pp. 1-24). Oxford & New York: Berg.

Jeffrey, L (1989). Writing and Rewriting Poetry: William Wordsworth. In D.B. Wallace & H.E. Gruber (Eds.), *Creative people at work: twelve cognitive case studies*. (pp. 69-89). New York: Oxford University Press.

Jones, E. (1998). *Acting*. London: Teach Yourself.

Jones, J. (1971). *On Aristotle and Greek Tragedy*. London: Chatto & Windus.

Juilliard. (n.d.). Drama 335-6 Performance Projects 1. In *Drama B.F.A (Acting Curriculum: Third-Year Performance Projects* (para. 1). Retrieved March 7 from, http://catalog.juilliard.edu/preview_program.php?catoid=17&poid=2032&returnto=1905

King. J. (Executive Producer). (2004, 26 January). *The Greatest Australian* [Television Program]. Sydney, NSW: Australian Broadcasting Commission.

Kirby, M. (2002). On acting and non-acting. In P.B. Zarrilli (Ed.), Acting *(Re)Considered: a theoretical and practical guide*. 2nd ed. (pp.40-60). London & New York: Routledge.

Koestler, A. (1970). *The Act of Creation*. London: Pan Books.

Komparu, K. (1983). *The Noh Theater: Principles and Perspectives*. New York & Tokyo: Weatherhill/Tankosha.

Konijn, E. (1995). Actors and emotions: a psychological perspective. *Theatre Research International, 20* (2), 132-140.

—. (2002). The Actor's Emotions Reconsidered: a psychological task-based perspective. In P.B. Zarrilli (Ed.), *Acting (Re)Considered: a theoretical and practical guide*. 2nd ed. (pp. 62-80). London & New York: Routledge.

Lassiter, L. (2002). David Warrilow: creating symbol and cypher. In P.B. Zarrilli (Ed.), Acting *(Re) Considered: a theoretical and practical guide*. 2nd ed. (pp.311-318). London & New York: Routledge.

Lavie, S., Narayan, K., & Ronaldo, R. (Eds.). (1983). *Creativity/Anthropology*. Ithaca & London: Cornell University Press.

Lecoq, J. (2002). *The Moving Body: Teaching Creative Theatre*. (D. Bradby, Trans.). London: Methuen.

Lee, K. (1993). Transcendence as an Aesthetic Concept: Implications for Curriculum. *Journal of Aesthetic Education 27* (1), 75-82.

Lewes, G.H. (1957). *On Actors and the Art of Acting*. New York: Grove Press. (Original work published in 1875)

Lowe, L. (2007). Toward 'Critical Generosity': cultivating student audiences. *Theatre Topics 17* (2), 141-151.

Lubart, T.I. (1999). Creativity across Cultures. In R.J. Sternberg (Ed.), *Handbook of Creativity.* (pp. 339-350). Cambridge: Cambridge University Press.

Macaulay, A. (2003). *Don't tell me, show me: directors talk about acting.* Sydney: Currency Press.

MacKinnon, D.W. (1976). Creativity: a multi-faceted phenomenon. In J.R. Wills (Ed.), *The Director in a Changing Theatre.* (pp. 250-261). Palo Alto: Mayfield.

Mackintosh, I. (1993). *Architecture, Actor and Audience.* London & New York: Routledge.

Marowitz, C. (1997). Grotowski in Irvine: Breaking the Silence. In R. Schechner & L. Wolford (Eds.), *The Grotowski Sourcebook.* (pp. 350-355). London & New York: Routledge.

Martindale, C. (1995). Creativity and Connectionism. In S.S. Smith, T.B. Ward & R.A. Finke (Eds.), *The Creative Cognition Approach.* (pp. 249-268). Cambridge, Mass. & London: MIT Press.

Masakazu, Y. (1984). The Aesthetics of Ambiguity: the artisitic theories of Zeami. In J.T. Rimer & Y. Masakazu. (Eds.), *On the Art of No Drama.* (pp.xxix-xlv) Princeton: Princeton University Press.

Mayer, R.E. (1999). Fifty Years of Creativity Research. In R.J. Sternberg (Ed.), *Handbook of Creativity.* (pp. 449-460). Cambridge: Cambridge University Press.

Melrose, L. (1989). *The Creative Personality and the Creative Process: a phenomenological perspective.* Lanham: University Press of America.

Merlin, B. (2007). *The Complete Stanislavsky Toolkit.* London: Nick Hern.

Nowra, L. (2004, July 24-25). Louis Nowra: Patrick, Judy and Me. *Weekend Australian Magazine.* pp. 18-21.

Pashler, H.E. (1998). *The Psychology of Attention.* Cambridge, Mass., & London: MIT Press.

Piirto, J. (2005). The Creative Process in Poets. In J.C. Kaufman & J. Baer (Eds.), *Creativity across Domains: Faces of the Muse.* (pp. 1-22). Mahwah & London: Lawrence Erlbaum.

Plucker, J.A. (2005). The (Relatively) Generalist View of Creativity. In J.C. Kaufman & J. Baer (Eds.), *Creativity across Domains: Faces of the Muse.* (pp. 307-312). Mahwah & London: Lawrence Erlbaum.

Plucker, J.A., & Renzulli, J.S. (1999). Psychometric Approaches to the Study of Human Creativity. In R.J. Sternberg (Ed.), *Handbook of Creativity.* (pp. 35-61). Cambridge: Cambridge University Press.

Privette, G. (1983). Peak Experiences, Peak Performance and Flow: A Comparative Analysis of Positive Human Experiences. *Journal of Personality and Social Psychology 45* (6), 1361-68.

Riley, J. (1997). *Chinese theatre and the actor in performance.* Cambridge: Cambridge University Press, 1997.

Roach, J.R. (1985). *The Player's Passion: studies in the science of acting.* London & Toronto: Associated University Press.

Rothenberg, A., & Greenberg, B. (1976). *The Index of Scientific Writings on Creativity (1566-1974).* Hamden, CT: Shoe String Press.

Rudlin, J., & Paul, N.H. (Eds.). (1990). *Jacques Copeau, Texts on Theatre.* London & New York: Routledge.

Russell-Parks, S.M. (1989). *A Phenomenological Analysis of the Actor's Perceptions during the Creative Act.* Florida State University, Tallahassee.

Saint-Denis, M. (1982). *Training for the Theatre: Premises and Promises.* New York & London: Theatre Arts Books & Heinemann.

Sawyer, R.K. (2005). Acting. In J.C. Kaufman & J. Baer (Eds.), *Creativity across Domains: Faces of the Muse.* (pp.41-55). Mahwah & London: Lawrence Erlbaum.

Schechner, R. (1993). Foreword: East and West and Eugenio Barba. In I. Watson, *Towards a Third Theatre: Eugenio Barba and the Odin Teatret.* (pp. vii-vx). London & New York: Routledge.

Seton, M. (2004). *Forming (In) Vulnerable Bodies: Intercorporeal Experiences in Actor Training in Australia.* University of Sydney, Sydney.

Simonton, D.K. (2005). Creativity in Psychology: on becoming and being a great psychologist. In J.C. Kaufman & J. Baer (Eds.), *Creativity across Domains: Faces of the Muse.* (pp.139-151). Mahwah & London: Lawrence Erlbaum.

—. (2004). *Creativity in Science: chance, logic, genius, and zeitgeist.* Cambridge & New York: Cambridge University Press.

Smith, S.M., Ward, T.B., & Finke, R.A. (Eds.). (1995). *The Creative Cognition Approach.* Cambridge, Mass: MIT Press.

Stanislavski, C. (1963). *An Actor's Handbook*: *an alphabetical arrangement of concise statements on aspects of acting.* (E. R. Hapgood, Ed. & Trans.). New York: Theatre Arts Book.

—. *An Actor Prepares.* (1964). (E.R. Hapgood, Trans.). New York: Routledge.

—. *Building a Character* (1977). (E.R. Hapgood, Trans.). New York: Routledge.

—. *Creating a Role.* (1961). (E.R. Hapgood, Trans.). New York & London: Routledge.

—. *My Life in Art.* (1952). (J. J. Robbins, Trans.). New York: Theatre Arts Books. (Original work published in 1924)

—. *Stanislavski's Legacy.* (1968). (E.R. Hapgood, Ed. & Trans.). London: Methuen.

Stanislavsky, K. (1973). Introduction. *On the Art of the Stage.* 2nd ed. (D. Magarshack, Trans.). London: Faber.

Sternberg, R. J. (2003). *Wisdom, intelligence, and creativity synthesized.* Cambridge: Cambridge University Press.

Sternberg, R.J., & Lubart, T.I. (1996). Investing in creativity. *American Psychologist, 51,* 677-688.

—. The Concept of Creativity: Prospects and Paradigms. (1999). In R.J. Sternberg (Ed.), *Handbook of Creativity.* (pp. 3-15). Cambridge: Cambridge University Press.

Sternberg, R.J., & O'Hara, L.A. (1999). Creativity and Intelligence. In R.J. Sternberg (Ed.), *Handbook of Creativity.* (pp. 251-272). Cambridge: Cambridge University Press.

Steyn, M. (1991, February 17). Sad, Perfunctory, Mechanical. *The New Criterion.* Retrieved August 9, 2004, from http://www.newcriterion.com/archive/17/feb99/steyn.htm.

Strasberg, L. (1989). *A Dream of Passion: the development of the Method.* London: Methuen.

—. (1957). Introduction. *The Paradox of Acting.* (pp. ix-xiv). (W.H. Pollock, Trans.). New York: Hill & Wang, 1957.

Strindberg, A. (1976). Preface. *Miss Julie.* (M. Meyer, Trans.). London: Eyre Methuen. (Original work published 1888)

Swede, G. (1993). *Creativity: a new psychology.* Toronto: Wall & Emerson.

Szeps, H. (1996). *All in Good Timing.* Sydney: Currency Press.

Taylor, G. (1989). *Players and Performances in the Victorian Theatre.* Manchester & New York: Manchester University Press.

Thomson, P. (2000). *On Actors and Acting.* Exeter: University of Exeter Press.

Toporkov, V.O. (1998). *Stanislavsky in Rehearsal: the final years.* (C. Edwards, Trans.). New York & London: Routledge/Theatre Arts Book. (Original work published 1954)

Trengrove, K. (1991). *Out of Character.* Melbourne: Penguin Books.

Turner, V. (1982). *From Ritual to Theatre: the human seriousness of play.* New York: PAJ.

Wallace, D.B., & Gruber, H.E. (Eds.). (1989). *Creative people at work: twelve cognitive case studies.* New York: Oxford University Press.

—. (1999). The case study method and evolving systems approach for understanding unique creative people at work. In R. J. Sternberg (Ed.), *Handbook of Creativity.* (pp. 93-115). Cambridge: Cambridge University Press.

Wallas, G. (1926). *The Art of Thought.* New York: Harcourt, Brace & Company.

Watson, I. (1993). *Towards a Third Theatre: Eugenio Barba and the Odin Teatret.* London & New York: Routledge.

Weiner, R.P. (2000). *Creativity and Beyond: Cultures, Values, and Change.* Albany: State University of New York Press.

Weisberg, R.W. (1986). *Creativity: Genius and Other Myths.* New York: Freeman.

Western Australian Academy of Performing Arts. (2001). *Advanced Diploma of Performing Arts (Acting).* Perth: Western Australian Academy of Performing Arts.

Whitehead, A.N. (1929). *Process and Reality: an essay in cosmology.* Cambridge: Cambridge University Press.

—-. (1920). The Method of Extensive Abstraction. In *The Concept of Nature.* (pp. 74-98). Cambridge: Cambridge University Press.

Williams, R. (1976). *Keywords: a Vocabulary of Culture and Society.* Glasgow: Fontana.

Woodward, C.E. (1989). Art and Elegance in the Synthesis of Organic Compounds. In D.B. Wallace & H.E. Gruber (Eds.), *Creative people at work: twelve cognitive case studies.* (pp. 227-254). New York: Oxford University Press.

Worthen, W.B. (1983). Stanislavsky and the Ethos of Acting. *Theatre Journal, 35* (1), 32-40.

—-. (1984). *The Idea of the Actor: Drama and the Ethics of Performance.* Princeton: Princeton University Press.

Zarrilli, P.B. (Ed.). (2002). *Acting (Re)Considered: a theoretical and practical guide.* 2nd ed. London & New York: Routledge.

—-. (2009). *Psychophysical Acting: an intercultural approach after Stanislavski.* London & New York: Routledge.

Zeami. 1984. The Nine Treatises. *On the Art of No Drama.* (pp. 3-256). (J. Thomas & Y. Masakazu, Trans.). Princeton: Princeton University Press.

Zinder, D. (2009). *Body Voice Imagination.* 2nd ed. London & New York: Routledge.

Zola, E. (1959). In H. Hennings & R.J. Judson Niess (Eds.) *Salons / Émile Zola: recueillis, annotés et presents.* Geneva: Droz & Paris: Minard.

Index